a b c d e f g h i j k l m n o p q r s t u v w x y z

The Usborne
First
Dictionary
with over 700 Internet links

Rachel Wardley and Jane Bingham
Designed by Susie McCaffrey
Assistant designer: Sue Grobecker

Illustrated by Teri Gower
and Stuart Trotter
Photography by Mark Mason Studio

Advisors: John McIlwain,
Rita D'Apice Gould, Peggy Porter Tierney

Finding a word

The words in a dictionary are arranged in alphabetical order from A to Z . This helps you to find them easily.

1 To find a word, such as "feeling", think of its first letter, "f."

2 Now look at the alphabet at the bottom of each page. When you see the letter "f" in a triangle, you have found the pages of "f" words.

3 Next, think of the second letter of your word. Look at the top of the page for words that begin "fe."

4 Then look down the "fe" words until you find your word.

Your word may not be in this dictionary, or you may have spelled it wrong. Spelling boxes, such as this one, will help you spell difficult words.

> **Some words that begin** with an "f" sound, such as **photograph**, are spelled "**ph.**"

Looking at a word

This dictionary tells you lots of things about words and how to use them.

You can check how to spell a word.

You can see other ways of using the word.

You can find out what the word means.

stretch
stretches stretching stretched
1 If you **stretch** something, you make it longer or bigger. *Sam stretched the rubber band until it snapped.*
2 When you **stretch**, you push your arms up or out as far as they will go. *Miriam stretched up high.*

You can see if a word has more than one meaning.

You can see how the word is used.

More help with words

Here are some ways that this dictionary helps you with writing, saying and understanding words.

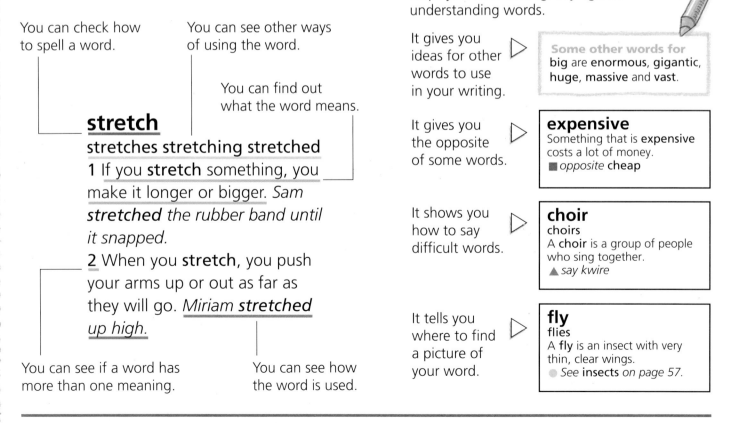

It gives you ideas for other words to use in your writing.

> **Some other words for** big are **enormous, gigantic, huge, massive** and **vast.**

It gives you the opposite of some words.

> **expensive**
> Something that is **expensive** costs a lot of money.
> ■ *opposite* **cheap**

It shows you how to say difficult words.

> **choir**
> **choirs**
> A **choir** is a group of people who sing together.
> ▲ *say kwire*

It tells you where to find a picture of your word.

> **fly**
> **flies**
> A **fly** is an insect with very thin, clear wings.
> ● *See* **insects** *on page 57.*

Alphabetical order

It's much easier to use a dictionary if you know how to put words into alphabetical order. See if you can do the Alphabetical animals quiz at the bottom of this page. Remember, to put words into alphabetical order, you compare their first letters, then their second letters, then their third, and so on.

For example, you put the words **bed**, **ant**, **bedtime**, **bead**, **bedroom** and **bad** into alphabetical order like this:

ant	*a comes before* b
bad	b*a comes before* b*e*
bead	bea *comes before* bed
bed	be*d comes before* bedr
bedroom	bed *comes before* bedr
bedtime	bedr *comes before* bedt

Alphabetical animals quiz

Can you put the names of these animals into alphabetical order? The answers are on page 144.

crocodile

chimpanzee

bear

chicken

crab

caterpillar

beaver

You could write your own list of words and put them in order.

Internet links

Some of the words in this dictionary have a symbol next to them, like this:

flower

This means there is a Web site where you can find out more about that subject or do an activity. For a link to this Web site, and to all the other Web sites recommended in this book, go to **www.usborne-quicklinks.com** and enter the keywords "first dictionary". On the Usborne Quicklinks Web site you will also find downloadable picture puzzles that you can print out to practice your spelling and punctuation.

Internet safety

Before you use the Internet, ask an adult to read through these safety guidelines with you.

● Always ask an adult's permission before you connect to the Internet.

● When you are on the Internet, never give out any personal information, such as your full name, address or telephone number.

● If a Web site asks you to log in or register by typing in your name or e-mail address, ask permission of an adult first.

Note to parents

We recommend that children are supervised while on the Internet, that they do not use Internet Chat Rooms, and that you use Internet filtering software to block unsuitable material. Please ensure that your children read and follow the safety guidelines printed above. Usborne Publishing is not responsible for the content of any Web site other than its own.

a b c d e f g h i j k l m n o p q r s t u v w x y z

Which meaning?

Which is the correct meaning for each of these words? Look up the words in your dictionary to see if you were right.

dessert
- ◆ A dessert is a large piece of dry land.
- ◆ A dessert is someone who feels lonely.
- ◆ A dessert is a sweet food.

mysterious
- ◆ Something that is mysterious cannot be found.
- ◆ If it is mysterious, the weather is very bad.
- ◆ If something is mysterious, it is hard to explain or understand.

infectious
- ◆ Food that is infectious does not taste very nice.
- ◆ If a disease is infectious, you can catch it from another person.
- ◆ If something is infectious, it is very important.

nephew
- ◆ Someone's nephew is their sister's or brother's son.
- ◆ Someone's nephew is their mother's brother.
- ◆ Someone's nephew is their sister's or brother's daughter.

Which word?

Your dictionary will help you to answer these questions. Check your answers in the dictionary or on page 144.

1 What is a small, furry animal and something that moves things on a computer screen?
Look on page 73.

2 What creature has fins, scales and a tail?
Find out in the letter "f."

3 What is the opposite of deep?
See page 32.

4 What other words can you use instead of big?
See page 15.

5 What is a hard rock and a small glass ball?
Think of a word beginning with "m."

6 How many shapes can you think of?
Look at page 106.

7 What has handlebars, a headlight and an engine?
Look at the words beginning with "m."

8 Bongos and maracas are both kinds of what?
See page 75.

9 What other words can you use instead of bad?
See page 12.

What am I?

Words that rhyme end with the same sound, so sad rhymes with bad and dish rhymes with fish. To find the answers to these clues, think of a word that rhymes with the one that you are given. The answers are on page 144.

I fly in the sky and I rhyme with fight.

I fit on your finger and I rhyme with sing.

You breathe me and I rhyme with pear.

You ride me and I rhyme with like.

You read me and I rhyme with look.

USING WORDS

This dictionary shows you lots of ways of using words. Here is a list of different kinds of writing and the pages where you can find them.

Dear Simon,
You wouldn't believe how hot it is here! The ocean is amazingly clear and blue and we've been swimming every day. I've collected lots of shells and seen some really strange creatures in the rock pools.
See you soon,
Kate

POSTCARD

Simon Small
12 Hilltop Road
Bridgeport, CT 06608

Adding words

Can you fill in the missing words in this story? Choose from the words in the box. You can read the completed story on page 144.

pebbles   top   heavy   drink   reach   bottom   pitcher   stream   thirsty   dropped   beak   work   idea

One hot day, a _thirsty_ crow called Caspar was searching for something to drink. The _stream_ had dried up and there was no water anywhere.

In the distance, Caspar saw a _Pitcher_ on a table outside a cottage. He flew over to have a look. "Ah, there's water at the _bottom_" he said. But he could not _Reach_ it. Caspar felt more and more thirsty. He tried to push over the pitcher, but it was so _heavy_ that he could not move it.

Then he had an _idea_ . He flew off to a pile of pebbles and picked one up in his _beak_. Caspar flew back, _dropped_ a pebble into the pitcher and then went off to find another. He dropped so many _Pebbl_ into the pitcher that they pushed the water up to the _top_ . At last, he could have a long, cool _drink_ . "All my hard _work_ was worth it in the end," thought clever Caspar.

Aa

able
If you are **able** to do something, you know how to do it. *Zack is able to ride a bike.*

about
1 **About** means to do with something. *This book is about elephants.*
2 **About** also means near to something. *Jo has about 15 birthday cards.*

above
If something is **above** another thing, it is over it. *The balloons floated above the fair.*
■ opposite
below

abroad
When you go **abroad**, you go to another country.

absent
If someone is **absent**, they are not here. *Donna was absent from school today.*

accident
accidents
1 If there is an **accident**, something bad happens that you do not expect. *Bonnie had an accident and broke her leg.*
2 If something happens by **accident**, nobody has planned or expected it. *I met my friend Peter by accident.*

ache
aches aching ached
If part of your body **aches**, it hurts. *Skating makes my legs ache.*
▲ rhymes with cake

acrobat
acrobats
Acrobats do amazing jumps and tricks, such as somersaults. *Acrobats often work in circuses.*

across
If you walk **across** the road, you go from one side to the other.

act
acts acting acted
1 When you **act**, you do something. *Marco acted quickly to put out the fire.*
2 If you **act** in a play, you pretend to be one of the people in it.

add
adds adding added
1 If you **add** something to another thing, you put it with that thing. *Add butter to the flour.*
2 When you **add** numbers, you put them together. *Jane added five and seven.*

address
addresses
Your **address** is the name of the place where you live.

Ms. Mandy Moss
12 Princess Street
Alexandria, VA 22103

admire
admires admiring admired
If you **admire** someone or something, you think that they are very nice or very good. *Joe admired Rachel's painting.*

adopt
adopts adopting adopted
When people **adopt** a child, the child comes to live with them and becomes part of their family.

adult
adults
An **adult** is a grown-up person.

adventure
adventures
An **adventure** is something exciting that people do. Some adventures can be dangerous. *Exploring the castle was a great adventure.*

advertise
advertises advertising advertised
When you **advertise** something, you make people notice it. *The children made a sign to advertise the school bake sale.*

afford
affords affording afforded
If you can **afford** something, you have enough money to buy it.

afraid
If you are **afraid**, you think something bad will happen. *Jessie is afraid that Mike will fall out of the tree.*

after

1 When one thing happens **after** another, it happens later. *We went for a walk **after** lunch.*
◼ **opposite before**
2 **After** also means following something. *William ran **after** the ball.*

afternoon

afternoons
The **afternoon** is part of the day. It starts at 12 o'clock and ends around 6 o'clock.

again

If you do something **again**, you do it one more time. *Beth is singing that song **again**.*

against

1 If you are **against** someone, you are on a different side from them. *The teams will play **against** each other tomorrow.*
2 If something is **against** another thing, it is next to it and touching it. *Bill leaned his bike **against** the wall.*

age

ages
Your **age** is how old you are.

ago

Ago means before now. *We started school two weeks **ago**.*

agree

agrees agreeing agreed
If you **agree** with someone, you both think the same about something. *Garth and I agreed that the movie was exciting.*

ahead

If you are **ahead** of someone, you are in front of them. *Kim ran on **ahead** of the others. Susie is **ahead** of Sasha in math.*

air

Air is what you breathe. You cannot see air but it is all around you.

aircraft

aircraft
An **aircraft** is any machine that flies.

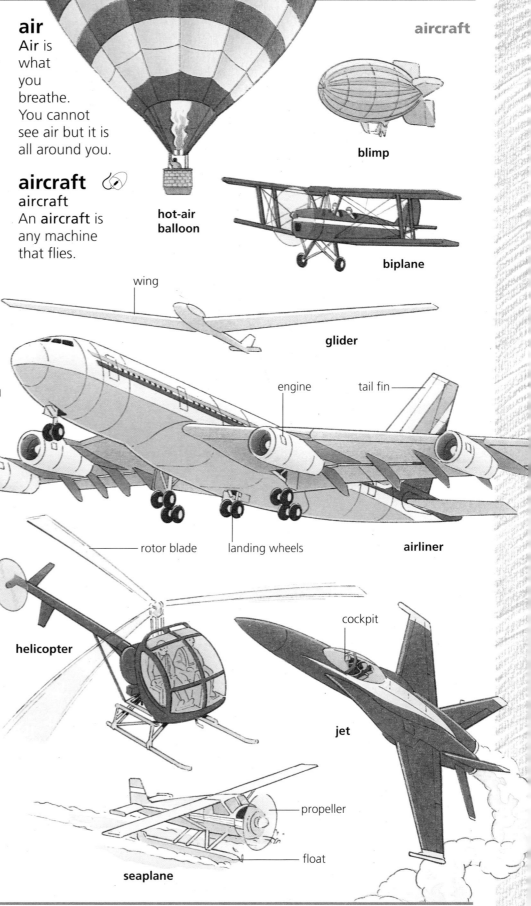

aircraft

blimp

hot-air balloon

biplane

wing

glider

engine

tail fin

rotor blade

landing wheels

airliner

helicopter

cockpit

jet

propeller

float

seaplane

A B C D E F G H I J K L M N O P Q R S T U V W X Y Z

airplane *to* **an**chor
8

For Internet links, go to
www.usborne-quicklinks.com

airplane
airplanes
An **airplane** is a large machine that flies through the air. Airplanes have wings and engines. They carry people and things.

airport
airports
An **airport** is a place where aircraft take off and land.

album
albums
An **album** is a book with blank

pages. You can stick photographs, stamps or pictures in an album.

alien
aliens
In stories, an **alien** is someone or something that comes from another planet. *Four aliens climbed out of the spacecraft.*

alike
If people are **alike**, they look or act the same. *The twins are alike.*

alive
If a person, an animal or a plant is **alive**, they are living.
■ *opposite* **dead**

all
All means everything, everyone, or the whole thing. *All the children were excited. Karen ate all the chocolate.*

alligator
alligators
An **alligator** is a reptile that looks like a crocodile, but has a flatter head and a shorter nose.

allow
allows allowing allowed
If someone **allows** you to do something, they let you do it. *Mom allowed us to stay up late.*

all right
Something that is **all right** is good enough. *Does this hat look all right?*

almost
Almost means close to. *It's almost bedtime.*

alone
When you are **alone**, you are not with anyone else.

along
1 If you walk **along** a street, you walk from one end of it to the other.
2 If you bring something **along**, you bring it with you. *Lee always brings his dog along when we go out together.*

aloud
When you read **aloud**, you read so that other people can hear you. *Nicki is reading her poem aloud.*

alphabet
alphabets
An **alphabet** is a set of all the letters that people use to write words. The letters in an alphabet are in a special order.

already
If something has happened **already**, it has happened before now. *I've seen this movie already.*

also
You use the word **also** to mean something extra. *Hannah ate an apple. She also ate my banana.*

always
If you **always** do something, you do it all the time or every time. *I always read before I go to sleep.*
■ *opposite* **never**

amazing
Something that is **amazing** is very surprising. *Dan showed us an amazing trick.*

ambulance
ambulances
An **ambulance** is a special vehicle that takes sick people to the hospital.

amount
amounts
An **amount** is how much there is of something. *Jessica ate a tiny amount of ice cream.*

anchor
anchors
An **anchor** is a heavy, metal hook on a long chain that is attached to a ship. When the anchor is thrown off a ship, it sinks to the bottom of the ocean and stops the ship from moving.

angry
angrier angriest
If you are **angry**, you feel upset and you often want to shout or fight with someone. *Kim was angry when she saw her broken glasses.*

animal
animals
An **animal** is anything that moves and breathes. Horses, lizards, fish, birds and insects are all animals. Plants are not animals.

ankle
ankles
Your **ankle** is the joint between your leg and your foot.

annoy
annoys annoying annoyed
If someone or something **annoys** you, they make you feel angry. *Ed annoyed his brother by singing.*

another
You use the word **another** to mean one more. *Please may I have another banana?*

answer
answers
An **answer** is what you say after someone has asked you a question. *Luis gave the right answer to the question.*

ant
ants
An **ant** is an insect. Ants live in large groups in the ground or in trees. *Some ants bite leaves from trees and carry them back to their nest.*

any
1 You use the word **any** to show that it does not matter which one. *Take any book you like.*
2 **Any** also means some. *Are there any cookies left?*

apart
1 **Apart** means away from something else. *Stand with your feet apart.*
2 If you take something **apart**, you take it to pieces. *Ben is taking his bike apart to see how it works.*

ape
apes
An **ape** is a large animal with long arms and no tail. Apes can walk and stand like human beings.

apologize
apologizes apologizing apologized
When you **apologize**, you say you are sorry for something that you have done or said. *Danny apologized for breaking the chair.*

appear
appears appearing appeared
When something **appears**, it can be seen. *Two birds appeared from inside the hat.*
■ opposite **disappear**

apple
apples
An **apple** is a rounded fruit with a green, red or yellow skin.

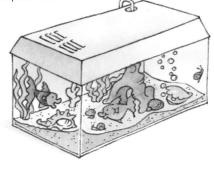

apron
aprons
You wear an **apron** to keep your clothes clean when you are cooking or painting.

aquarium
aquariums
An **aquarium** is a glass tank filled with water. You keep fish and other creatures in an aquarium.

area
areas
An **area** is a place or a space. *A science area. A large area of grass.*

aren't
Aren't is a short way of saying **are not**. *These strawberries aren't ripe yet.*

A B C D E F G H I J K L M N O P Q R S T U V W X Y Z

argue
argues arguing argued
People **argue** because they do not
agree about something. When
they argue, they say what they
think and often get angry. *We*
argued about which team was
the best.

argument
arguments
You have an **argument** when you
do not agree with someone.
When people have an argument
they say what they think and often
get angry.

arm
arms
Your **arm** is the part of your body
between your shoulder and your
hand.

armchair
armchairs
An **armchair** is
a comfortable
chair with
parts on
either side for
you to rest
your arms on.

armor
Armor is a set of clothes made of
metal. Soldiers wore armor long
ago to protect themselves when
they were fighting.

army
armies
An **army** is a large group of
people who fight in a war.

around
1 **Around** means in a circle. *Mo*
tied a ribbon ***around*** *her waist.*
2 **Around** also means in every
part. *I looked* ***around*** *the house.*
3 **Around** can also mean near to
something. *Kit lives* ***around*** *here.*

arrange
arranges
arranging
arranged
1 If you
arrange
things, you
put them
together
so that
they look
tidy or pretty.
Rita is ***arranging*** *some flowers.*
2 When you **arrange** something,
you plan how it will be done.
Mom is ***arranging*** *a party for*
next weekend.

arrive
arrives arriving arrived
When something or someone
arrives, they get to where they are
going. *The package* ***arrived*** *at*
Carla's house. We ***arrived*** *at*
the soccer game on time.

arrow
arrows
1 An **arrow** is a thin stick with a
point at one end and feathers at
the other end. You shoot arrows
from a bow.
2 An **arrow** is also a sign that
shows you which way to go.
Follow the ***arrows*** *to get to the*
sports hall.

art
Art is something beautiful that has
been made by someone. Paintings
and drawings are types of art.

ask
asks asking asked
1 If you **ask** a question, you say
that you want to know something.
Jim ***asked*** *me how old I was.*
2 If you **ask** for something, you
say that you want it. *Kerry* ***asked***
for an apple.

asleep
When you
are **asleep**,
your eyes are
closed and
your whole
body is resting.
Pickles is ***asleep*** *on a cushion.*

assembly
assemblies
An **assembly** is a large group of
people who are meeting together.
School ***assembly***.

astonish
astonishes astonishing
astonished
If you **astonish** someone, you
make them feel very surprised.

astronaut
astronauts
An **astronaut** is someone who
goes into space. Astronauts travel
in spacecraft.

astronaut

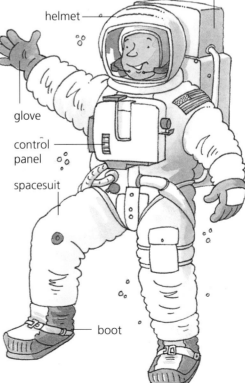

air tank

helmet

glove

control
panel

spacesuit

boot

a b c d e f g h i j k l m n o p q r s t u v w x y z

ate

Ate comes from the word **eat**.
Usually we eat at home. Yesterday we ate at a restaurant.

atlas

atlases
An **atlas** is a book of maps.

attach

attaches attaching attached
When you **attach** one thing to another, you join them together. *Tim attached the leash to Fido's collar.*

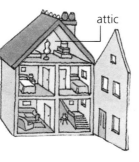

attack

attacks attacking attacked
If someone **attacks** another person, they try to hurt them.

attention

When you pay **attention**, you watch and listen carefully. *Pay attention to what I'm saying!*

attic

attics
An **attic** is a room at the top of a house, just under the roof.

attic

attract

attracts attracting attracted
When a magnet **attracts** an object, it makes it come nearer.

audience

audiences
An **audience** is a group of people who watch or listen to something, such as a play or a piece of music.

aunt

aunts
Your **aunt** is the sister of your mom or your dad. Your uncle's wife is also your aunt. Another word for aunt is auntie.

autumn

Autumn is one of the four seasons of the year. It comes between summer and winter. In the autumn, it begins to get cold and leaves fall from the trees. Autumn is also called fall.
say aw-tum

awake

Awake means not asleep. *Owls stay awake at night and sleep in the day.*

awful

Something that is **awful** is very bad. *An awful meal.*

awkward

1 Something that is **awkward** is difficult to use. *The heavy baseball bat was awkward for little Joe to swing.*
2 Someone who moves in an **awkward** way is clumsy.
3 If you feel **awkward**, you are shy and don't know what to do or say.

ax

axes
An **ax** is a tool with a long handle and a large, metal blade. People use axes to chop wood.

baby

babies
A **baby** is a very young child.

baby sitter

baby sitters
A **baby sitter** is someone who looks after children when their parents are out.

back

backs
1 The **back** of something is the part farthest from the front. *We sat at the back of the theater.*
■ opposite front
2 Your **back** is the part of your body between your neck and your bottom.

backward

1 If a word is spelled **backward**, it is spelled the wrong way around. "Step" spelled backward is "pets."
2 If you move **backward**, you move the way that your back faces. *Todd is walking backward through the snow.*
■ opposite forward

back yard

back yards
A **back yard** is an area at the back of a house where you can play or grow plants.

bad
worse worst
1 Someone who is **bad** does things that they should not do.
■ *opposite* **good**
2 Something that is **bad** is not good. *A **bad** movie.*
■ *opposite* **good**

> **Some other words for**
> **bad** are awful, terrible and lousy.

badge
badges
A **badge** is a small picture that you wear on your clothes.

badger
badgers
A **badger** is a black and white animal that lives underground.

bag
bags
You use a **bag** to hold or carry things. *A shopping **bag**.*

bake
bakes baking baked
When you **bake** food, you cook it in an oven.

balance
balances balancing balanced
If you **balance** something, you keep it steady so that it does not fall. *Mom balanced a ball on her nose.*

bald
balder baldest
People who are **bald** have no hair on the top of their heads.

ball

balls
A **ball** is a round object that you throw and catch.

ballet
Ballet is a kind of dance with special steps, that you do to music. **Ballet** often tells a story.
▲ *say bal-ay*

balloon
balloons
A **balloon** is a thin, rubber bag. When you blow into a balloon, it gets bigger.

banana
bananas
A **banana** is a long, curved fruit with a thick, yellow skin.

band
bands
1 A **band** is a group of people who play music together.
2 A **band** is also a strip that you put around something. *Alice is wearing a hair **band**.*

bandage
bandages
A **bandage** is a strip of cloth or plastic that you put over a part of your body that has been hurt.

bang
bangs banging banged
If something **bangs**, it makes a sudden, loud noise. *The door banged in the wind.*

bank
banks
1 A **bank** is a safe place where people can keep their money. Banks sometimes lend money to people.
2 A **bank** is also the ground beside a river or a stream. *The goose stood on the **bank**.*

bar
bars
A **bar** is a long, thin piece of wood or metal.

barbecue
barbecues
A **barbecue** is a meal that is cooked outside on a fire.

bare
barer barest
1 If you are **bare**, you are not wearing any clothes.
2 If a shelf is **bare**, it has nothing on it.

bark

Bark is the hard skin that covers a tree's trunk and branches.

bark

barks
barking
barked

When a dog **barks**, it makes a loud noise in its throat.

barn

barns

A **barn** is a large farm building. Straw, animals and machines are kept in barns.

baseball

baseballs

1 **Baseball** is a game played by two teams using a bat and a ball.
2 A **baseball** is the hard, white ball that you use to play baseball.

basket

baskets

You use a **basket** to carry things. Baskets can be made from strips of wood, wire or string.

basketball

basketballs

1 **Basketball** is a game played by two teams using a large ball. Each team tries to throw the ball through a net, called a basket.
2 A **basketball** is the large, rubber ball that you use to play basketball.

bat

bats

1 A **bat** is a small, furry animal with wings. Bats sleep during the day and hunt for food at night.
2 A **bat** is also a kind of stick that you use to hit a ball.

bath

baths

When you take a **bath**, you sit in a tub that is filled with water and wash yourself.

battery

batteries

A **battery** is a tube or a box that makes electricity. You put batteries into flashlights, toys and radios to make them work.

be

is being was been

1 **Be** means to live or to take up space. *I want to **be** by the ocean.*
2 The word **be** also shows what something is like. *I used to **be** shy.*

beach

beaches

A **beach** is a strip of sand or stones by the edge of a lake or an ocean.

bead

beads

A **bead** is a small object with a hole through its middle. You can make necklaces with beads.

beak

beaks

A **beak** is the hard outside part of a bird's mouth.

bean

beans

A **bean** is a small vegetable. Beans often grow in pods.

bear

bears

A **bear** is a large, wild animal with thick fur. *Some **bears** catch fish to eat.*

beard

beards

A **beard** is the hair that grows on a man's chin and cheeks.

beat

beats beating
beat beaten

1 If you **beat** someone in a race or a contest, you do better than they do.
2 If you **beat** something, you keep hitting it. *Stuart **beat** his drum.*

beautiful

If something is **beautiful**, it is nice to look at or listen to.

beaver

beavers

A **beaver** is an animal that lives in or near a river. It has very sharp teeth and a large, flat tail.

became

Became comes from the word **become**. *I hope the weather will become sunnier. Yesterday, it **became** sunny in the afternoon.*

because

You use the word **because** to explain why something happens. *I was scared **because** it was dark.*

become

becomes becoming became become

If one thing **becomes** something else, it changes into it. *Some caterpillars **become** butterflies.*

bed

beds

A **bed** is something that you lie on when you sleep or rest.

bedroom

bedrooms

Your **bedroom** is the room where you sleep.

bedtime

bedtimes

Your **bedtime** is the time when you go to bed.

bee

bees

A **bee** is an insect with black and yellow stripes on its body. Some bees make honey.
● *See **insects** on page 57.*

beef

Beef is meat that comes from a cow.

beetle

beetles

A **beetle** is an insect with four wings. It has two soft wings that it uses for flying and two hard wings that protect its body.
● *See **insects** on page 57.*

before

If something happens **before** something else, it happens first.
■ *opposite* **after**

begin

begins beginning began begun

When you **begin** to do something, you start to do it. *Jo **began** to cry.*

behave

behaves behaving behaved

1 The way you **behave** is the way that you do things. *Annie is **behaving** very strangely today.*
2 If you **behave** yourself, you are good.

behind

If you are **behind** something, you are at the back of it. *Naomi hid **behind** the shed.*

believe

believes believing believed

If you **believe** something, you think that it is true. *You shouldn't **believe** Bud's stories.*

bell

bells

A **bell** is a metal object shaped like a cup. Bells make a ringing noise when you hit them or shake them.

belong

belongs belonging belonged

1 If something **belongs** to you, it is yours. *This hat **belongs** to me.*
2 If you **belong** to a club, you are a member of it.
3 If something **belongs** in a place, that is where it should be. *The shovel **belongs** in the shed.*

below

If something is **below** another thing, it is under it. *Katy sank **below** the surface of the water.*
■ *opposite* **above**

belt

belts

A **belt** is a thin band of leather, cloth or plastic that you wear around your waist. *Henry's **belt** keeps his pants from falling down.*

bench

benches

A **bench** is a long, hard seat.

bend

bends bending bent

If something **bends**, it changes its shape so that it is not straight. *These straws **bend** in the middle.*

beneath

If something is **beneath** another thing, it is below it. *Spot is hiding **beneath** the table.*

bent

Bent comes from the word **bend**. *Grandma could not bend low enough to pick up her letters, so Honey **bent** down to get them.*

berry

berries

A **berry** is a small, soft fruit. *Mom makes jelly from **berries**.*

beside

If you are **beside** someone or something, you are next to them. *I sit **beside** Sam at school.*

best

Something that is the **best** is better than all the others. *Jan won a prize for doing the **best** painting.*
■ *opposite* **worst**

a **b** c d e f g h i j k l m n o p q r s t u v w x y z

better

1 You use the word **better** to mean very good compared with something else. *My bike is **better** than yours.*
2 If you feel **better**, you do not feel ill any more.

between

If you are **between** two things, you are in the middle of them.

beware

The word **beware** tells you to be careful because something is dangerous. *Beware of the bull.*

bicycle

bicycles
A **bicycle** is a vehicle with two wheels. You push the pedals to turn the wheels.

bicycle
seat
handlebars
tire
pedal
chain

big

bigger biggest
A **big** person or thing is large.
■ *opposite* small

Some other words for

big are **enormous, gigantic, huge, massive** and **vast.**

---

bike

bikes
Bike is short for **bicycle**.

bill

bills
A **bill** is a piece of paper money.

bird

birds
A **bird** is a creature with two wings. Birds have a beak and are covered with feathers. Most birds can fly.

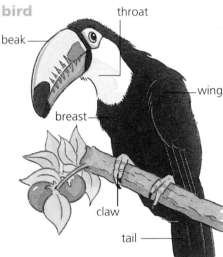

bird
throat
beak
wing
breast
claw
tail

birthday

birthdays
Your **birthday** is the date that you were born. People give you gifts each year on your birthday.

biscuit

biscuits
A **biscuit** is a kind of bread roll. Some people eat biscuits for breakfast.

bite

bites biting bit bitten
When you **bite** something, you cut into it with your teeth. *Jenny **bit** into a pear.*

bitter

If something tastes **bitter**, it has a strong, sour taste. Orange peel tastes bitter.

black

Black is a color. The letters on this page are black.

blackboard

blackboards
A **blackboard** is a black surface that you can write on with chalk.

blade

blades
A **blade** is the flat, sharp part of a knife that is used for cutting. Scissors have two blades.

blame

blames blaming blamed
If you **blame** someone, you think that they have made something bad happen. *Alexander **blamed** his brother for breaking his model airplane.*

blank

A **blank** piece of paper has nothing on it.

blanket

blankets
A **blanket** is a thick cover. You can put blankets on your bed to keep you warm.

bleed

bleeds bleeding bled
If you **bleed**, blood comes out of your body. *Kenny's nose **bled** when he bumped into the door.*

blew

Blew comes from the word **blow**. *Kim can blow very hard. She **blew** out all the candles on her cake.*

blind

Blind people cannot see.

blink
blinks blinking blinked
When you **blink**, you close and then open your eyes very fast.

block
blocks
A **block** is a thick piece of something, such as wood or stone. Blocks usually have straight sides. *Building* **blocks**.

block
blocks blocking blocked
If something **blocks** the way, nothing can get past. *A fallen tree has* **blocked** *the road.*

blood
Blood is the red liquid inside your body. Your heart pushes blood through your body.

blouse
blouses
A **blouse** is a piece of clothing. Women and girls wear blouses on the top part of their bodies.

blow
blows blowing blew blown
1 When you **blow**, you push air out of your mouth. *Amy* **blew** *hard to put out all the candles.*
2 When the wind **blows**, it moves the air. *The wind has* **blown** *away dad's newspaper.*

blue
Blue is a color. The sky on a sunny day is blue.

blunt
blunter bluntest
Something that is **blunt** is not sharp. *A* **blunt** *knife.*

board
boards
A **board** is a flat piece of wood or cardboard. *A chess* **board**.

boast
boasts boasting boasted
Someone who **boasts** enjoys telling other people about what they have done or about the things that they own. *Annie is* **boasting** *about her new bike.*

boat
boats
A **boat** travels on water. It carries people or things across rivers, lakes and seas. Some boats have engines and some have sails.

boats

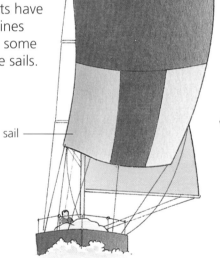

sailboat

inflatable dinghy

mast

rudder

sailing dinghy

sail

speedboat   engine

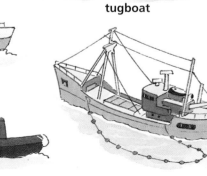

tugboat

yacht

ferry

houseboat

fishing boat

For Internet links, go to

www.usborne-quicklinks.com
17
body *to* **bo**ttom

body

bodies

The **body** of a person or an animal is every part of them. Your legs, shoulders and head are all parts of your body.

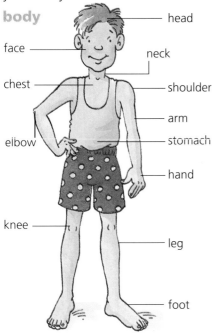

body — head
face — neck
chest — shoulder
— arm
elbow — stomach
— hand
knee — leg
— foot

boil

boils boiling boiled

1 When water **boils**, it becomes very hot. There are bubbles in the water and steam rises from it.
2 When you **boil** food, you cook it in boiling water.

bone

bones

Your **bones** are the hard parts inside your body. Skeletons are made of bones.

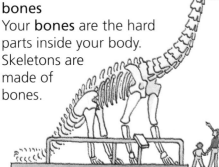

bonfire

bonfires

A **bonfire** is a large fire that is lit outdoors.

book

books

A **book** is a group of pages placed inside a cover. The pages can have writing or pictures on them.

book report

book reports

When you write a **book report**, you say what you think of a book that you have read.

THE VAMPIRE WHO HATED THE DARK

The vampire who hated the dark

This is a very funny book about a timid vampire called Victor. I like the part when Victor runs away from his shadow, but I think the picture

could be more exciting. My favorite character is Victor's mom because she puts spiders in his soup.

Some children might be frightened by this book, but I really enjoyed it.

boot

boots

A **boot** is a kind of shoe that covers your foot and part of your leg. People wear boots in bad weather.

bored

If you are **bored**, you are annoyed because you have nothing to do.

born

When a baby is **born**, it comes out of its mother.

borrow

borrows borrowing borrowed

If you **borrow** something, someone lets you have it for a short time. *I borrowed Jo's hat.*

both

Both means two together. *Keep both hands on the handlebars.*

bottle

bottles

Bottles hold liquid. They are made from glass or plastic.

bottom

bottoms

1 The **bottom** is the lowest part of something.
2 Your **bottom** is the part of your body that you sit on.

bought

Bought comes from the word
buy. *We always buy Mom a
birthday present. Last year, we
bought her some flowers.*

bounce

bounces
bouncing
bounced

When something **bounces,**
it springs back after hitting
another thing. *The ball
bounced off Hannah's head.*

bow

bows

1 A **bow** is a knot with two loops.
You tie your shoelaces in a bow.
2 A **bow** is also a curved piece of
wood with a string stretched from
one end to the other. You use a
bow to shoot arrows.
3 You also use a **bow** to play the
violin. A bow is made from a long
piece of wood with hair stretched
from one end to the other.
● *See* **musical instruments**
on page 74.

bowl

bowls

You use a **bowl** to
hold food or drink.
Bowls are usually round.

box

boxes

You use a **box** to keep things in.
Boxes usually have straight sides.

boy

boys

A **boy** is a male child.

bracelet

bracelets

A **bracelet** is a chain or band that
you wear around your wrist.
● *See* **jewelry** *on page 59.*

brain

brains

Your **brain**
is inside your
head. You
use your brain
to think and
to make your
body work.

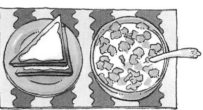

brain

brake

brakes

You use the **brakes** on a car or a
bike to make it slow down or stop.

branch

branches

A **branch** is part of a tree.
Branches grow from the trunk of
a tree.

brave

braver bravest

If you are **brave,** you are not
afraid to do something
frightening. *Ellie was **brave** about
staying in the hospital.*

bread

Bread is a food that is made with
flour and baked in an oven.

break

breaks breaking broke broken

1 When something **breaks,** it
splits into pieces. *The
mug broke when
Anna dropped it.*
2 When a
machine **breaks,**
it stops working.
*Scott broke
my radio.*

breakfast

breakfasts

Breakfast is the
first meal of the day.

breathe

breathes breathing breathed

When you **breathe,** you suck air
into your body and then let it out
again. You can breathe through
your nose or your mouth.

breeze

breezes

A **breeze** is a gentle wind.

brick

bricks

A **brick** is a block of baked clay.
Bricks are used for building.

bridge

bridges

A **bridge** is something that is built
over a river, a road or a railroad
so that people can
get across.

bright

brighter brightest

1 Something that is **bright** gives
out a lot of light. *The sun is very
bright.*
2 A **bright** color is strong and
easy to see. *Jenny wore a **bright**
pink sweater.*

a **b** c d e f g h i j k l m n o p q r s t u v w x y z

bring
brings bringing brought
If you **bring** something, you take it with you. *Bring some money.*

broad
broader broadest
Something that is **broad** is very wide. *A broad river.*

broke
Broke comes from the word **break**. *I tried not to break the vase, but it broke into lots of pieces.*

broken
If something is **broken**, it is damaged or it does not work. My radio is *broken*.

broom
brooms
A **broom** is a brush with a long handle. You use a broom to sweep up dirt from a floor or leaves from a path.

brother
brothers
Your **brother** is a boy who has the same mom and dad as you have.

brought
Brought comes from the word **bring**. *Lucy often brings something interesting to school. Last week, she brought her pet snake.*

brown
Brown is a color. Wood and chocolate are brown.

bruise
bruises
A **bruise** is a purple mark on your skin. You get a bruise when part of your body is hit by something. *Sam has a bruise on his knee where he knocked it.*

brush
brushes

A **brush** has lots of hairs or wires attached to a handle. You use a brush to neaten your hair and paint pictures.

bubble
bubbles
A **bubble** is a ball of liquid that is filled with air. There are bubbles in boiling water.

bucket
buckets

You use a **bucket** to hold or carry things. A bucket has a flat bottom, curved sides and a handle.

build
builds building built
If you **build** something, you make it by putting things together. *Craig is building a model plane.*

building
buildings
A **building** is a place with walls and a roof. Houses, stores, schools and offices are buildings.

built
Built comes from the word **build**. *Juanita won our contest to build the tallest tower. She built one that was three feet high.*

bulb
bulbs
1 A **bulb** is the part of a plant that is under the ground. Flowers, such as daffodils and crocuses, grow from bulbs.
2 A light **bulb** lights up when you turn on a light. Bulbs are made of glass.

bulb

bull
bulls
A **bull** is a male cow. Bulls have horns.

bulldozer
bulldozers
A **bulldozer** is a large machine that moves rocks and soil.

bully
bullies
A **bully** is someone who tries to hurt or frighten other people.

bump
bumps
A **bump** is something round that sticks out. *Osman has a bump on his head.*

bump
bumps bumping bumped
If you **bump** into something, you hit it without meaning to. *Osman bumped into a shelf.*

bunch

bunches

A **bunch** is a group of things. *A bunch of flowers. Bunches of grapes.*

bunk beds

Bunk beds are two beds that are joined together, one above the other.

burglar

burglars

A **burglar** is someone who breaks into a building and steals things.

burn

burns burning burned burned

1 If you **burn** something, you set it on fire. *We burn logs in our fireplace.*

2 **Burn** also means to damage something with fire or heat. *Nakisha has burned the toast.*

3 If you **burn** yourself, you touch something that is hot and get hurt.

burst

bursts bursting burst

When something **bursts**, it breaks apart suddenly. *The bag burst and scattered apples all over the floor.*

bury

buries burying buried

If you **bury** something, you hide it in the ground. *The pirates buried the treasure under a tree.*

bus

buses

A **bus** is a large vehicle that carries lots of people. *Terry travels to school by bus.*

bush

bushes

A **bush** is a plant with lots of branches. Bushes are smaller than trees.

busy

busier busiest

Busy people have a lot of things to do.

butcher

butchers

A **butcher** is someone who sells meat.

butter

Butter is a yellow food that is made from milk. You can spread butter on bread or use it for cooking.

butterfly

butterflies

A **butterfly** is an insect with four large wings.

See **insects** *on page 57.*

button

buttons

A **button** is a small object that is sewn onto clothes. Buttons fit into buttonholes to fasten clothes together.

buy

buys buying bought

When you **buy** something, you pay money so that you can have it. *Eugene bought a kite from the toy store.*

■ *opposite* **sell**

Cc

cabbage

cabbages

A **cabbage** is a round vegetable with a lot of leaves. Cabbages can be green, white or purple.

caboose

The **caboose** is the last car on a train.

café

cafés

A **café** is a place with tables and chairs. You buy and eat drinks and snacks in a café.

▲ *say kaf-ay*

cage

cages

A **cage** is a box or a room with bars. Some pets and zoo animals are kept in cages.

cake

cakes

A **cake** is a sweet food that is baked in an oven. Cakes are made with eggs, flour, sugar and butter.

calculator

calculators

A **calculator** is a machine that gives you math answers.

calendar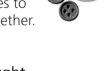

calendars

A **calendar** is a list of all the days, weeks and months in a year. *Tiffany marked her birthday on the calendar.*

a **b c** d e f g h i j k l m n o p q r s t u v w x y z

calf
calves

A **calf** is a baby cow. Baby seals, elephants, giraffes and whales are also called calves.

call
calls calling called

1 If you **call** someone, you shout to them so that they come to you. *Dad* **called** *us to come inside for dinner.*
2 When you **call** someone something, you give them a name. *Marvin* **called** *his kitten Pepper.*
3 **Call** also means to telephone. *David* **calls** *his uncle every week.*

calm
calmer calmest

If you are **calm**, you feel peaceful.

came

Came is from the word **come**. *Henry comes to stay with us every summer. Last year, he* **came** *in August.*

camel
camels

A **camel** is a large animal with one or two humps on its back. Camels carry people and things across deserts.

camera
cameras

A **camera** is a machine that you use to take photographs.

camp
camps camping camped

When you **camp**, you live in a tent for a short time.

can
cans

A **can** is a metal container with curved sides. *A* **can** *of soup.*

can
could

If you **can** do something, you are able to do it. *Oscar* **can** *juggle.*

candle
candles

A **candle** is a stick of wax with a string through the middle. When a candle burns, it makes light.

candy
candies

Candy is a sweet food made from sugar and other ingredients, such as chocolate or nuts. *What is your favorite* **candy**?

cannot

If you **cannot** do something, you are not able to do it. *Megan* **cannot** *swim.*

canoe
canoes

A **canoe** is a narrow, light boat that you move with paddles.
▲ *say kan-oo*

can't

Can't is a short way of saying **cannot**. *Megan* **can't** *swim.*

cap
caps

A **cap** is a soft hat with a peak at the front.

capital
capitals

1 A **capital** is the main city of a country or a state. Country or state leaders work in the capital. *The* **capital** *of Texas is Austin.*
2 A **capital** is a big letter of the alphabet, such as R or Z. You use a capital when you begin writing a sentence or a name.

car
cars

1 A **car** is a machine with four wheels and an engine. People travel from place to place in cars.

car   windshield
hood
headlight   bumper
tire

2 A **car** is also a part of a train. Cars are pulled by an engine and people sit in them. Trains usually have lots of cars.

card
cards

1 A **card** is a piece of stiff paper with writing on it. *A library* **card**.
2 A greeting **card** is a folded piece of stiff paper. It has a picture on the front and a message inside. You send cards to people at special times, such as birthdays
3 Playing **cards** are pieces of stiff paper with numbers or pictures on them. You play games with playing cards.

cardboard

Cardboard is very thick, strong paper. It is used for making boxes.

cardigan

cardigans

A **cardigan** is a kind of knitted sweater that opens at the front.

care

cares caring cared

1 If you **care** for a person or an animal, you look after them. *Mario has two rabbits and he cares for them himself.*
2 If you **care** about something, you think that it is important. *Amy cares about the way she looks.*

careful

If you are careful, you think about what you are doing. *Ben was careful not to spill the drinks.*

careless

Someone who is **careless** does not think about what they are doing.

carpenter

carpenters

A **carpenter** is someone who makes or repairs the wooden parts of buildings. Carpenters make doors, shelves and stairs.

carrot

carrots

A **carrot** is a long, orange vegetable that grows under the ground. You can eat carrots raw or cooked.

carry

carries carrying carried

If you **carry** something, you take it somewhere with you. *Michael carried his bag to the station.*

carton

cartons

Cartons are used to hold food or drink. They are made from cardboard or plastic.

cartoon

cartoons

1 A **cartoon** is a filmstrip that tells a story using drawings.
2 A **cartoon** is also a funny drawing.

case

cases

You use a **case** to hold or carry things. *Timmy keeps his glasses in a case.*

cash

Cash is money in coins and bills.

cassette

cassettes

A **cassette** is a plastic case with a tape inside it. *A **video** cassette.*

castle

castles

A **castle** is a large building with high walls to keep enemies out. Most castles were built a long time ago.

cat

cats

A **cat** is a furry animal with a long tail. Cats are often kept as pets. Some cats, such as lions and tigers, are large and wild.

catch

catches catching caught

1 When you **catch** something, you take hold of it while it is in the air. *Jerry ran to catch the ball.*
2 If you **catch** a bus or a train, you get on it. *David caught the last bus home.*

caterpillar

caterpillars

A **caterpillar** is a small creature that looks like a worm with lots of short legs. Caterpillars turn into butterflies or moths.

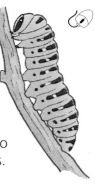

cattle

Cattle is a word for cows and bulls. *We saw some cattle in the fields.*

caught

Caught comes from the word **catch**. *Jerry ran to catch the ball. He caught it easily.*

cauliflower

cauliflowers

A **cauliflower** is a round vegetable. Cauliflowers have green leaves and a white center.

a b c d e f g h i j k l m n o p q r s t u v w x y z

For Internet links, go to
www.usborne-quicklinks.com
23
cave *to* **ch**ase

cave
caves

A **cave** is a large hole in the side of a cliff or a mountain. There are also caves under the ground.

CD
CDs

CD is short for **compact disc**.

ceiling
ceilings

The **ceiling** is the part of a room that is above your head. Lights hang from ceilings.

▲ *say* **see**-ling

cellar
cellars

A **cellar** is a room under a house.

cement
Cement is a gray powder that is mixed with water and gets very hard when it dries. People use cement to make sidewalks.

center
centers

The **center** of something is the middle of it.

centipede
centipedes

A **centipede** is a small creature with a very long body and lots of legs.

century
centuries

A **century** is a period of one hundred years.

cereal
cereals

1 **Cereals** are farm plants such as wheat or rice. Their seeds are used for food.
2 **Cereal** is also the name for foods that you eat with milk at breakfast time.

certain
If you are **certain** about something, you are sure about it. *Robert is **certain** that his team will win.*

certificate
certificates

A **certificate** is a piece of paper which says that you have done something. *A cycling **certificate**.*

chain
chains

A **chain** is a row of metal rings that are joined together.

chair
chairs

A **chair** is a seat with four legs and a back. Chairs are made for one person to sit on.

chalk
chalks

Chalk is a soft rock. It can be made into sticks that you use to write and draw.

champion
champions

A **champion** is the winner of a race or a contest.

chance
chances

1 If you have a **chance** to do something, you can do it soon. *Peter has the **chance** to go skiing.*
2 If something happens by **chance**, it has not been planned. *I met my friend by **chance**.*

change
Change is the money that is given back to you when you pay too much for something.

change
changes changing changed

1 When you **change** something, you make it different. *Billy **changed** the date of his party.*
2 When you **change**, you put on different clothes. *Sally **changed** before she went out.*

chapter
chapters

A **chapter** is a part of a book. *That book has 12 **chapters**.*

character
characters

1 A **character** is a person in a story, a movie or a play.
2 Your **character** is the sort of person you are.

charge
If someone is in **charge** of something, they organize it. *Aunt Jane is in **charge** of the picnic.*

charge
charges charging charged

If someone **charges** you for something, they ask you to pay money for it.

chart
charts

A **chart** is a picture, a map or a list that shows things clearly.

chase
chases chasing chased

If you **chase** someone, you run after them and try to catch them.

*Sidney is **chasing** Emily.*

cheap
cheaper cheapest
Something that is **cheap** does not cost much.
■ *opposite* **expensive**

cheat
cheats cheating cheated
If you **cheat**, you break the rules so that you can win or get something that you want.

check
checks checking checked
If you **check** something, you make sure that it is right. *Lola **checked** the spelling of "sword" in her dictionary.*

checkers
Checkers is a game for two people. You play checkers by moving pieces across a board of black and red squares.

cheek
cheeks
Your **cheeks** are the soft sides of your face.

cheerful
Someone who is **cheerful** feels happy or seems happy.

cheese
cheeses
Cheese is a food that is made from milk. Cheese can be hard or soft.

cherry
cherries
A **cherry** is a small, round fruit with a pit in the center. Cherries can be red, black or yellow.

chess
Chess is a game for two people. You play chess by moving special pieces, such as a queen or a knight, across a board of black and white squares.

chest
chests
1 Your **chest** is the front part of your body between your neck and your waist.
2 A **chest** is a large, strong box that you keep things in. Chests are usually made of wood.

chew
chews chewing chewed
When you **chew** food, you bite it lots of times before you swallow it.

chick
chicks
A **chick** is a very young bird.

chicken
chickens
1 A **chicken** is a bird that is kept on a farm.
2 **Chicken** is also a kind of meat that comes from chickens.

child
children
A **child** is a young boy or girl.

chimney
chimneys
A **chimney** is a wide pipe above a fire that carries smoke out of a building.

chimpanzee
chimpanzees
A **chimpanzee** is an ape with dark fur. Chimpanzees can be quite clever.

chin
chins
Your **chin** is the part of your face below your mouth.

chip
chips
A **chip** is a small snack food. Chips are often made from potatoes.

chip
chips chipping chipped
If you **chip** something, you break off a small piece of it by accident.

chocolate
chocolates
Chocolate is a sweet food that is used to make candy, cakes and drinks.

choir
choirs
A **choir** is a group of people who sing together.
▲ *say kwire*

choose
chooses choosing chose chosen
If you **choose** something, you pick out the thing that you want. *Dave is **choosing** a shirt.*

chop
chops chopping chopped
If you **chop** something, you cut it into pieces with a knife or an ax.

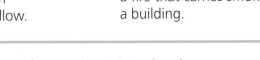

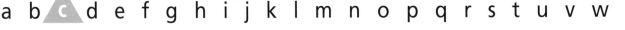

a b **c** d e f g h i j k l m n o p q r s t u v w x y z

chopsticks

Chopsticks are long, thin sticks that people use to pick up food. *Do you know how to eat with chopsticks?*

chosen

Chosen comes from the word **choose**. *It's Dan's turn to choose what we will do. He has **chosen** a trip to the fair.*

chunk
chunks

A **chunk** is a thick piece of something. *Mom cut me a **chunk** of cheese.*

cider
ciders

Cider is a drink that is made from apples.

circle
circles

A **circle** is a round shape.
● *See* **shapes** *on page 106.*

circus
circuses

A **circus** is a kind of show. Acrobats, clowns and jugglers do tricks in circuses.

city
cities

A **city** is a very big place where many people live and work. Cities are larger than towns.

clap
claps clapping clapped

When you **clap**, you make a loud noise by slapping your hands together. People clap to show that they have enjoyed something, such as a play or a concert.

class
classes

A **class** is a group of people who are taught together. *We are in Mrs. Gould's **class** this year.*

classroom
classrooms

A **classroom** is a room in a school where children have lessons.

claw
claws

A **claw** is one of the sharp, curved nails on the feet of some birds and animals. Eagles, crocodiles and cats have claws.

clay

Clay is a kind of dirt. When clay is wet, it can be made into different shapes. When it dries or is baked, it becomes hard. *Kate made a pot out of **clay**.*

clean
cleans cleaning cleaned

When you **clean** something, you remove the dirt from it. *Pete needs to **clean** his boots.*

clean
cleaner cleanest

Something that is **clean** does not have any dirt on it. *Marco wore a **clean** shirt to the party.*
■ *opposite* **dirty**

clear
clearer clearest

1 If a thing is **clear**, you can see through it. *Clear plastic.*
2 Something that is **clear** is easy to understand. *The directions were **clear** and easy to follow.*

clever
cleverer cleverest

If you are **clever** at something, you are good at doing it. *Josie is **clever** at writing stories.*

cliff
cliffs

A **cliff** is a hill with one very steep side. You often see cliffs near the edge of the ocean.

climb
climbs climbing climbed

When you **climb** something, you move up it. People sometimes use their hands and feet to climb.

cloak
cloaks

A **cloak** is a loose coat without sleeves.

clock
clocks

A **clock** is a machine that shows you what time it is.

close
closes closing closed

If you **close** something, you shut it. *Close the door behind you.*
▲ *say* kloze
■ *opposite* **open**

close
closer closest

If something is **close**, it is near. *Stay **close** to me.*
▲ *say* kloze

closet
closets
A **closet** is a very small room where you keep your clothes.

cloth
Cloth is material that is used to make clothes and other things.

clothes
Clothes are things that you wear, such as shirts, socks and jeans.

cloud
clouds
Clouds are white or gray shapes that you see in the sky. They are made of tiny drops of water.

clown
clowns
A **clown** is someone who makes people laugh. Clowns wear funny clothes and do tricks.

club
clubs
A **club** is a group of people who meet together because they enjoy doing the same thing.

clue
clues
A **clue** is something that helps you to find the answer to a question. *The police need some clues to help them find the burglar.*

clumsy
clumsier clumsiest
Clumsy people are not very careful about the way they move and often knock things over.

clutch
clutches clutching clutched
If you **clutch** something, you hold onto it tightly. *Zachary clutched his friend's arm to stop himself from falling.*

coach
coaches
1 A **coach** is someone who teaches you to play a sport. *A basketball coach.*
2 A **coach** is also a vehicle that is pulled by horses. Before cars were invented, people used coaches.

coal
Coal is a black rock that is found under the ground. It makes heat when you burn it.

coast
coasts
The coast is the land that is next to the ocean.

coat
coats
1 A **coat** is a piece of clothing that you wear over your other clothes. Coats have long sleeves and are usually made from thick material.
2 An animal's **coat** is the fur or hair that covers its body. *Fido has a long, thick coat.*

cobweb
cobwebs
A **cobweb** is a very thin net that a spider makes. Spiders use their cobwebs to catch insects.

cocoon
cocoons
A **cocoon** is a case made from threads, where a caterpillar lives while it turns into a butterfly.

coin
coins
A **coin** is a round, flat piece of metal. Coins are used as money.

cold
colds
When you have a **cold**, your nose runs and you cough and sneeze a lot.

cold
colder coldest
1 If something is **cold**, it is not hot. *A cold drink.*
■ *opposite* **hot**
2 If the weather is **cold**, the temperature is low. *It was so cold that Jim shivered.*
■ *opposite* **hot**

collar
collars
1 The **collar** of a shirt or a jacket is the part of it that fits around your neck.
2 A **collar** is also a band that goes around the neck of a dog or a cat.

collect
collects collecting collected
1 When you **collect** things, you put them together. *I collect shells.*
2 If you **collect** something, you take it from a place. *José collected his mail from the box.*

college
colleges
A **college** is a place where people can learn after they have finished high school.

a b **c** d e f g h i j k l m n o p q r s t u v w x y z

color
colors
Red, yellow and blue are the main **colors**. You can make other colors by mixing the main ones.

colors

yellow

blue

red

orange

green

pink

purple

brown

white

black

comb
combs
A **comb** is a flat piece of plastic or metal with very thin teeth. You use a comb to make your hair tidy.

come
comes coming came come
When you **come** to a person or a thing, you move toward them.

comfortable
If something is **comfortable**, it feels good. *A comfortable chair.*

comic book
comic books
A **comic book** is a magazine with stories told in pictures.

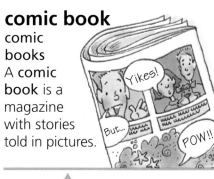

common
commoner commonest
Things that are **common** are ordinary and you see lots of them. *Computers are common in schools.*

compact disc
compact discs
A **compact disc** is a round piece of plastic with music or information stored on it. Compact discs are also called CDs. *Wayne is listening to his new compact disc.*

compare
compares comparing compared
When you **compare** two things, you look at them carefully to see if they are the same or different. *Lauren compared the dresses to decide which she liked best.*

compass
compasses

1 A **compass** is something that shows you which way you are facing. A compass has a needle which always points north.

2 A **compass** is also a kind of tool that you use to draw a circle.

complain
complains complaining complained
If you **complain** about something, you say that you are not happy about it.

complete
completes completing completed
When you **complete** something, you finish it. *Dana completed her homework and went out to play.*

complete
Something that is **complete** does not have anything missing. *Amy checked to make sure that the jigsaw puzzle was complete.*

computer
computers
A **computer** is a machine that works with words, numbers, pictures and sound. Computers can work very quickly. *Jake loves playing games on his computer.*

computer

screen

keyboard

mouse

concentrate
concentrates concentrating concentrated
When you **concentrate** on something, you think hard about it. *Jamel is concentrating on his game of chess.*

concert
concerts
When people give a **concert**, they play music or sing to an audience.

concrete
Concrete is a mixture of cement, small stones, sand and water. It becomes very hard when it dries. Concrete is used for building.

confuse
confuses confusing confused
If someone **confuses** you, they make it hard for you to understand something. *Travis confused me with his long words.*

connect
connects connecting connected
If you **connect** two things, you join them together.

consonant
consonants
A **consonant** is any letter of the alphabet except the vowels a, e, i, o and u. B and f are consonants.

contain
contains containing contained
1 If a box **contains** something, it has that thing inside it.
2 If a book **contains** some stories, the stories are in the book.

container
containers
A **container** is something that you use to keep things in. Boxes, bags and baskets are all containers.

contest
contests
When you take part in a **contest**, you see who is best at something. *Who won the drawing contest?*

control
controls controlling controlled
When you **control** something, you make it do what you want. *Al can control his toy car.*

conversation
conversations
When two people have a **conversation**, they talk to each other.

cook
cooks cooking cooked
When you **cook** food, you heat it until it is ready to eat. *Ed cooked a delicious meal.*

cookie
cookies
A **cookie** is a small, flat cake that is baked in an oven. *Mom baked cookies for my party.*

cool
cooler coolest
Something that is **cool** feels a little cold. *A cool breeze.*

copy
copies copying copied
If you **copy** someone, you do the same as they do. *Mitch is copying the way his dad walks.*

cord
cords
Cord is a type of string. Some bags have a cord around the top that you pull to close the bag.

corner
corners
A **corner** is a place where two sides join together. *We met at the the corner of the field.*

correct
If something is **correct**, it does not have any mistakes in it.

correct
corrects correcting corrected
1 When teachers **correct** your work, they check to see if there are any mistakes in it.
2 If you **correct** something, you make it right where it was wrong.

corridor
corridors
A **corridor** is a long passage inside a building or a train.

cost
costs costing cost
If something **costs** a certain amount of money, you can buy it for that much. *How much does that hat cost?*

costume
costumes
A **costume** is a set of clothes that you wear to make yourself look different. *Freddie wore a bear costume for the school play.*

cot
cots
A **cot** is a narrow bed that folds. *We sleep in cots when we go camping.*

cottage
cottages
A **cottage** is a small house. You usually see cottages in the country.

cotton
Cotton is soft and white and comes from a cotton plant. Cotton is made into thread and cloth.

couch
couches
A **couch** is a long, comfortable seat for two or more people.

cough
coughs coughing coughed
When you **cough**, you force air out of your throat with a sudden, loud noise. You often cough when you have a cold.
▲ *rhymes with off*

could
Could comes from the word **can**. *Manuel can juggle with four balls. Last month, he **could** only juggle with three.*

couldn't
Couldn't is a short way of saying **could not**. *Maggie **couldn't** swim before she had lessons.*

count
counts counting counted
1 When you **count**, you say numbers one after the other.
2 When you **count** a number of things, you add them up to find out how many there are. *I have **counted** all the jigsaw pieces.*

counter
counters
1 A **counter** is a long table in a store. Someone stands behind the counter and serves you.
2 A **counter** is also a small piece of plastic that you use in some games.

country
countries
1 A **country** is a part of the world with its own people and laws.
2 The **country** is the land outside towns and cities. There are fields, woods and farms in the country.

cousin
cousins
Your **cousin** is the son or daughter of your aunt or uncle.

cover
covers covering covered
If you **cover** something, you put something else over it. *Erin **covered** the cake with icing.*

cow
cows
A **cow** is a large farm animal. Cows are kept for their meat and their milk.

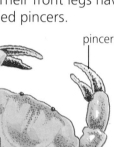

crab
crabs
A **crab** is a creature with a hard shell that lives in the ocean. Crabs have ten legs. Their front legs have large claws called pincers.

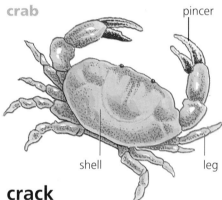

crab
pincer
shell
leg

crack
cracks
A **crack** is a line that shows where something has broken. *This mug has a **crack** in it.*

crane
cranes
A **crane** is a tall machine that lifts heavy loads.

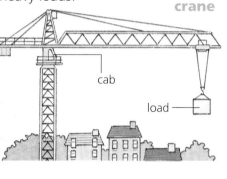

crane
cab
load

crash
crashes
A **crash** is a sudden loud noise. *The plates fell to the ground with a crash.*

crash
crashes crashing crashed
When something **crashes**, it hits something else and makes a sudden loud noise. *The car **crashed** into a tree.*

crawl
crawls crawling crawled
When you **crawl**, you move around on your hands and knees. *Abby **crawled** under the table to hide.*

crayon
crayons
A **crayon** is a colored pencil. Some crayons are made from wax.

cream
Cream is the thick part of milk. You can use cream in cooking or pour it over fruit or cereal.

creature
creatures
A **creature** is anything that moves and breathes. Horses, lizards, fish, birds and insects are all creatures.

creep
creeps creeping crept
If you **creep** somewhere, you move very slowly and quietly. *Jay **crept** past his sleeping brother.*

crew
crews
A **crew** is a group of people who work together on a boat or a plane.

A B **C** D E F G H I J K L M N O P Q R S T U V W X Y Z

cricket

crickets

A **cricket** is a jumping insect. Crickets make a noise by rubbing their wings together.

cried

Cried comes from the word **cry**. *Pattie began to cry. She **cried** for nearly an hour.*

crocodile

crocodiles

A **crocodile** is a reptile that lives in rivers in hot countries. Crocodiles have sharp teeth, short legs and a long tail.

crooked

Something that is **crooked** is not straight. *That picture looks crooked. This path is crooked.*

crop

crops

Crops are grown in fields and used for food. Wheat, potatoes and rice are crops.

cross

crosses

A **cross** is a sign that looks like +.

cross

crosses crossing crossed

When you **cross** a road, you go from one side of it to the other.

cross

crosser crossest

If you are **cross**, you are not pleased about something and you feel angry.

crossword

crosswords

A **crossword** is a word puzzle with clues. You work out the answer to a clue, then write the word in squares on the puzzle.

ACROSS

1 When you travel by plane, you ____.
3 The color of the sky on a sunny day.
6 A color and a fruit.
8 Clothes for your hands.
12 A drop of water from your eye.
13 An animal that you keep at home.
14 When you put two numbers together, you ____.

DOWN

1 Once a tadpole, now a ____.
2 A toy on a string.
4 Not on time.
5 Rain and snow are types of ____.
7 A bird's home.
9 One of the edges of your mouth.
10 Someone who takes care of animals.
11 Difficult, or not soft.

crowd

crowds

A **crowd** is a large group of people. *A football crowd.*

crown

crowns

A **crown** is a special kind of hat made from gold, silver and jewels. Kings and queens wear crowns.

cruel

crueller cruellest

Cruel people are mean and often hurt other people or animals.

crumb

crumbs

A **crumb** is a very small piece of dry food. *Cake crumbs.*

crust

crusts

The **crust** is the hard part on the outside of a pie or a loaf of bread. *Nathan never eats his crusts.*

a b **c** d e f g h i j k l m n o p q r s t u v w x y z

cry
cries crying cried
When you **cry**, tears come from your eyes. People cry when they are sad or hurt.

cube
cubes
A **cube** is a solid shape with six square sides. *Dice are cubes.*
● See **shapes** *on page 106.*

cucumber
cucumbers
A **cucumber** is a long, green vegetable that you eat in salads.

cuddle
cuddles cuddling cuddled
When you **cuddle** someone, you hold them closely in your arms.

cuff
cuffs
A **cuff** is the part of a shirt that fastens round your wrist.

cup
cups
You drink from a **cup**. Cups are usually round and have a handle on one side.

cupboard
cupboards
A **cupboard** is a place to keep food or dishes. Cupboards have shelves and a door.

cupcake
cupcakes
A **cupcake** is a small, round cake for one person.

curious
If you are **curious** about something, you want to find out about it. *Aaron was curious about the package.*

curl
curls
A **curl** is a piece of hair that is curved. *Becky has beautiful curls.*

curtain
curtains
A **curtain** is a piece of material that you pull across a window to cover it.

curve
curves
A **curve** is a line that bends.

cushion
cushions
A **cushion** is a kind of pillow. You use cushions to make sofas and chairs more comfortable.

custard
Custard is a sweet, yellow dessert made from eggs, milk and sugar.

customer
customers
A **customer** is someone who buys something in a store.

cut
cuts cutting cut
1 If you **cut** something, you use a knife or a pair of scissors to divide it into pieces. *Cut the card in half.*
2 When you **cut** yourself, something sharp pushes through your skin and makes you bleed.

Dd

dad
dads
Dad is a name for your father.

daily
If something happens **daily**, it happens every day. *Jacob practices the piano daily.*

dairy
dairies
A **dairy** is a place where milk is put into bottles or cartons. Food made from milk, such as cheese and yogurt, also comes from dairies.

daisy
daisies
A **daisy** is a flower with white petals and a yellow center.

damage
damages damaging damaged
If you **damage** something, you break it or spoil it.

damp
damper dampest
Something that is **damp** is a little bit wet. *The dew has made the grass damp.*

dance
dances dancing danced
When you **dance**, you move your body to music.

danger

Danger is something that could
happen to hurt you.

dangerous

If something is **dangerous**, it can
hurt or kill you.

dare

dares daring dared
If you **dare** to do something, you
are brave enough to do it. *Paulo*
dared to climb the tree.

dark

darker darkest
1 When it is **dark**, there is no
light or very little light.
2 **Dark** colors are not pale.
Dark blue.
■ *opposite* **light**

date

dates
When someone asks you
what **date** it is, you tell
them the month and the
day. *The date today is*
June 20th.

daughter

daughters
A **daughter** is somebody's
female child.

day

days
1 A **day** starts and ends at
midnight. There are 24 hours in
a day.
2 **Day** is the time when it is light
outside. *We've been out all day.*

dead

If a person, an animal or a plant is
dead, they are no longer living.
■ *opposite* **alive**

deaf

Deaf people cannot hear at all or
cannot hear very well.

dear

dearer dearest
1 If someone is **dear** to you, you
love them. *A dear friend.*
2 You use the word **dear** when
you begin a letter. *Dear Mrs. Bott.*

decide

decides deciding decided
When you **decide** to do
something, you make up your
mind to do it. *Maggie decided to*
wear her purple shorts.

deck

decks
A **deck** is a floor on a boat or
a ship.

decorate

decorates decorating
decorated
1 When you **decorate**
something, you add
things to it to make it
look prettier. *Milly*
***decorated** the hall*
for her party.
2 If you **decorate**
a room, you paint it or put
wallpaper on its walls.

deep

deeper deepest
Something that is **deep** goes
down a long way. *A deep well.*
■ *opposite* **shallow**

deer

deer
A **deer** is
an animal
with four
legs and
brown fur.
Deer
live in
woods and
can run very fast. Male deer have
big horns called antlers.

delicious

Food or drink that is **delicious**
tastes or smells very good.

deliver

delivers delivering delivered
If you **deliver** something, you take
it to somebody. *The mail carrier*
delivered a letter to Leigh.

dentist

dentists
A **dentist** is someone who takes
care of your teeth.

depth

depths
The **depth** of a thing is the
distance between its top and its
bottom. *We measured the depth*
of the pool.

describe

describes describing described
When you **describe** something,
you say what it is like. *José*
described his new house to me.

desert

deserts
A **desert** is a large piece of land
where very few plants grow.
Deserts are very dry and are often
covered with sand.

deserve

deserves deserving deserved
If you **deserve** a thing, you earn it
by doing something. *Tim **deserves***
a rest after all his hard work.

desk

desks
A **desk** is a kind of table that you
sit at to write.

dessert

desserts
A **dessert** is a sweet food that you
eat at the end of a meal. *Tanya*
*chose ice cream for **dessert**.*

a b c **d** e f g h i j k l m n o p q r s t u v w x y z

destroy

destroys destroying destroyed
Destroy means to damage something so badly that it cannot be mended. *The storm **destroyed** our toolshed.*

diagram

diagrams
A **diagram** is a drawing that shows something in a clear and simple way.

diamond

diamonds
1 A **diamond** is a jewel. Diamonds are clear and shiny.
2 A **diamond** is also a shape with four sides.
● *See* **shapes** *on page 106.*

diary

diaries
A **diary** is a book in which you write down things that happen to you each day.

dice

Dice are cubes with a different number of spots on each side. You use dice in some games.

dictionary

dictionaries
A **dictionary** is a book of words. Dictionaries tell you what words mean and show you how to spell them.

didn't

Didn't is a short way of saying did not. *Matt **didn't** like the movie.*

die

dies dying died
When a person, an animal or a plant **dies**, they stop living.

different

If a thing is **different**, it is not the same as something else.

difficult

If something is **difficult**, you need to try hard to do it.
■ *opposite* **easy**

dig

digs digging dug
When you **dig**, you make a hole in the ground. You usually dig with a shovel.

dinner

dinners
Dinner is a name for the biggest meal of the day.

dinosaur

dinosaurs
Dinosaurs were reptiles that lived a very long time ago. Some dinosaurs were very big and fierce.

dinosaurs

direction

directions
A **direction** is the way that you go to get to a place. *The station is in this **direction**.*

dirt

1 **Dirt** is mud or dust or anything that stops things from being clean.
2 Plants grow in the **dirt**.

dirty

dirtier dirtiest
If something is **dirty**, it has mud, food or other marks on it.
■ *opposite* **clean**

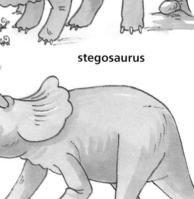

diplodocus

stegosaurus

tyrannosaurus rex

triceratops

A B C D E F G H I J K L M N O P Q R S T U V W X Y Z

disagree
disagrees disagreeing disagreed
If you **disagree** with someone,
you do not think the same as they
do about something. *We*
disagreed about the meal. Nina
thought it was good, but I
thought it was awful.

disappear
disappears
disappearing
disappeared
If something
disappears, you cannot
see it any more. *The sun*
disappeared behind a cloud.
■ *opposite* **appear**

disappointed
If you are **disappointed**, you are
sad because something has not
happened. *Jo was disappointed*
that her friend couldn't come.

disaster
disasters
A **disaster** is something
terrible that happens.

disc jockey
disc jockeys
A **disc jockey** is someone who
plays tapes and CDs at parties and
dances.

discover
discovers discovering
discovered
When you **discover** something,
you find out about it for the first
time. *Megan discovered that her*
friend had been lying.

discuss
discusses discussing discussed
When you **discuss** something, you
talk about it with someone else.
We discussed which way we
would go home.

disease
diseases
A **disease** is something that makes
you sick. Measles is a disease.

disguise
disguises
A **disguise** is something that you
wear to make you look like
someone else.

dish
dishes
You put food in a **dish**. Dishes are
usually round.

dishonest
Someone who is **dishonest** does
not tell the truth.
■ *opposite* **honest**

dishwasher
dishwashers
A **dishwasher** is a machine that
washes and dries dishes, glasses,
knives, forks and spoons.

disk
disks
A **disk** is a flat piece
of metal and plastic
that stores information
from a computer.

disobey
disobeys disobeying disobeyed
If you **disobey** someone, you do
not do what they tell you to do.
■ *opposite* **obey**

display
displays
A **display** is a group of things that
have been arranged for people to
look at. *An art display.*

dissolve
dissolves dissolving dissolved
When a tablet **dissolves** in water,
it mixes so well with water that
you cannot separate them easily.

distance
distances
The **distance** between two things
is the space between them. *We*
measured the distance between
the two tables.

disturb
disturbs disturbing disturbed
If you **disturb** someone, you stop
them from doing something
for a short time. *Bart keeps*
disturbing me when I am
trying to read.

dive
dives diving dived
When you **dive** into
water, you
jump in head
first, with
your arms
stretched out
in front of you.

divide
divides dividing divided
1 When you **divide** something,
you make it into smaller pieces.
Ed divided the cake into six pieces.
2 When you **divide** numbers, you
find out how many times one
number goes into another.
Helen divided 12 by 2.

doctor
doctors
A **doctor** is someone
who helps
sick people
to get
better.

doesn't

Doesn't is a short way of saying **does not**. *Jabar **doesn't** like cold weather.*

dog

dogs

A **dog** is an animal that is often kept as a pet. Some dogs are trained to do work.

doll

dolls

A **doll** is a toy that looks like a person.

donkey

donkeys

A **donkey** is an animal that looks like a small horse. Donkeys have long ears and a furry coat.

don't

Don't is a short way of saying **do not**. *I **don't** like strawberries.*

door

doors

You open a **door** to get into a building, a room or a closet.

double

Double means twice as big. *Your lollipop is **double** the size of mine.*

doubt

doubts doubting doubted

If you **doubt** something, you are not sure about it. *I **doubted** if Freddie's story was true.*
▲ say dowt

doughnut

doughnuts

A **doughnut** is a small cake which is covered with sugar. Doughnuts sometimes have jelly inside them.

down

When something moves **down**, it goes from a higher place to a lower place. *We rode our bikes **down** the hill.*
■ *opposite* up

drag

drags dragging dragged

If you **drag** something, you pull it along the ground. *Davina **dragged** her sled up the hill.*

dragon

dragons

A **dragon** is a fire-breathing monster that you read about in stories. Dragons have wings and a long tail.

drain

drains

A **drain** is a pipe that carries away liquids.

drama

When you do **drama**, you act and make up plays.

drank

Drank comes from the word **drink**. *Caitlin likes to drink milk. She **drank** three glasses this morning.*

drapes

Drapes are heavy curtains that you pull across a window to cover it. *Do you like our new **drapes**?*

draw

draws drawing drew drawn

When you **draw**, you use pencils or crayons to make a picture.

drawer

drawers

A **drawer** is a box that slides in and out of a piece of furniture. You use drawers to keep things in.

drawing

drawings

A **drawing** is a picture made with pencils or crayons.

drawn

Drawn comes from the word **draw**. *Laura likes to draw. She has **drawn** a picture of a house.*

dream

dreams

A **dream** is a story that you see and hear while you are sleeping. *I had a funny **dream** last night.*

A B C D E F G H I J K L M N O P Q R S T U V W X Y Z

dress
dresses
A **dress** looks like a skirt and a top joined together. Women and girls wear dresses.

dress
dresses dressing dressed
When you **dress**, you put on your clothes. *Billy dressed quickly.*

drew
Drew comes from the word **draw**. *We all had to draw our favorite food. I **drew** a bowl of ice cream.*

dried
Dried comes from the word **dry**. *We hung the clothes outside to dry. They had **dried** by lunch time.*

drill
drills
A **drill** is a tool that makes holes in hard surfaces.

drink
drinks drinking drank drunk
When you **drink**, you swallow liquid.

drip
drips dripping dripped
When something **drips**, drops of liquid fall from it. *The faucet is dripping.*

drive
drives driving drove driven
When someone **drives** a vehicle, they make it go somewhere.

drop
drops
A **drop** is a tiny amount of liquid. *Drops of rain.*

drop
drops dropping dropped
If you **drop** something, you let it fall. *Carly **dropped** her dinner on the floor.*

drove
Drove comes from the word **drive**. *Glenn drives a truck. He **drove** thousands of miles last month.*

drown
drowns drowning drowned
If someone **drowns**, they die because they are underwater and cannot breathe.

drum
drums
A **drum** is a hollow musical instrument with a thin skin stretched over each end. You hit the skin with sticks or with your hands.

drunk
Drunk comes from the word **drink**. *Amy drinks milk all the time. She has **drunk** six glasses already today.*

dry
dries drying dried
When you **dry** something, you take water out of it or off it. *Paul is **drying** the dishes.*

dry
drier driest
Something that is **dry** does not have any water in it or on it.
■ *opposite* **wet**

duck
ducks
A **duck** is a bird that can swim. Ducks have short legs and can dive under water.

dug
Dug comes from the word **dig**. *The pirates began to dig. They **dug** a hole to hide their treasure.*

dull
duller dullest
1 A **dull** color is not very bright.
2 Something that is **dull** is not very interesting. *A **dull** book.*

dungeon
dungeons
A **dungeon** is a prison under the ground. Dungeons are usually found in castles.

dust
Dust looks like powder and is made up of tiny, dry pieces of dirt. *The books were covered in **dust**.*

dustpan
dustpans
People use a **dustpan** and brush to sweep up crumbs and dust from floors.

dye
dyes dying dyed
When you **dye** something, you change its color by soaking it in a special liquid. *Mom has dyed my shirt purple.*

dying
Dying comes from the word **die**. *Plants die if you do not give them water. Our plants were **dying** when we came home.*

Ee

each
Each means every one. *Hal gave each puppy a name. The roses cost $2.00 each.*

eager
If you are **eager** to do something, you really want to do it. *Alexander is eager to learn to play the guitar.*

eagle

eagles
An **eagle** is a large bird with a curved beak and sharp claws. Eagles hunt small animals for food.

ear
ears
Your **ears** are the parts of your body that you use to hear.

early
earlier earliest
1 If you arrive **early**, you arrive before the time that you were expected. *Abby was early because her watch was wrong.*
2 **Early** also means near the beginning of something. *We set off early in the morning.*
■ *opposite* **late**

earn
earns earning earned
If you **earn** money, you work to get it. *Teri earned some money by working in her uncle's garden.*

earth

1 **Earth** is the planet that we live on.
2 Plants grow on the **earth**.

earthquake
earthquakes
When there is an **earthquake**, the ground shakes and buildings often fall down.

east
East is a direction. The sun rises in the east.

easy
easier easiest
If something is **easy**, you do not have to try hard to do it.
■ *opposite* **difficult**

eat
eats eating ate eaten
When you **eat**, you chew and swallow food. *Scott is eating his lunch.*

echo
echoes
An **echo** is a sound that you hear again and again. *Our voices made echoes in the cave.*
▲ *say* **ek-oh**

edge
edges
An **edge** is the place where something ends. *The glass fell off the edge of the table. We played at the edge of the pond.*

effect
effects
An **effect** is a thing that happens because of something else. *This spell has the amazing effect of turning a prince into a frog.*

effort
If you put **effort** into something, you try very hard at it. *Misha has put a lot of effort into her project.*

egg
eggs
Eggs contain young birds or insects which break out when they are ready to be born. People often eat hens' eggs.

either
Either means one or the other. *You can have either an apple or an orange.*

elbow
elbows
Your **elbow** is the joint in the middle of your arm, where it bends.

electricity
Electricity is a kind of energy that makes light and heat. Electricity is also used to make machines work.

elephant
elephants
An **elephant** is a very large animal with a long trunk and big ears.

A B C D E F G H I J K L M N O P Q R S T U V W X Y Z

elevator
elevators
An **elevator** is a small room that goes up and down. Elevators carry people between floors of a building.

empty
emptier emptiest
If something is **empty**, there is nothing inside it.
■ *opposite* **full**

encyclopedia
encyclopedias
An **encyclopedia** is a book that contains information about many different subjects.

end
ends
The **end** of something is its last part. *The **end** of the story. The **end** of the train.*

end
ends ending ended
If you **end** something, you finish it. *Bonnie **ended** the argument by walking out.*

enemy
enemies
Your **enemy** is someone who hates you and may want to hurt you.

energy
1 When you have **energy**, you have the strength to do things. *Mo is full of energy.*

2 **Energy** is also the power that makes machines work and produces heat and light.

engine
engines
1 An **engine** is a machine that makes things move or work. Cars, planes and ships have engines.

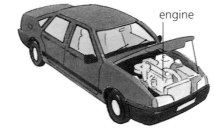

engine

2 An **engine** is also the front part of a train that pulls it along.

enjoy
enjoys enjoying enjoyed
If you **enjoy** something, you like doing it. *Akiko **enjoys** skating.*

enormous
Something that is **enormous** is very big. *Whales are **enormous**.*

enough
If you have **enough** of something, you have as much as you need. *Have you had **enough** lunch?*

enter
enters entering entered
When you **enter** a place, you go into it.

entrance
entrances
An **entrance** is a way into a place. *We searched for the **entrance** to the secret passage.*
■ *opposite* **exit**

envelope
envelopes
An **envelope** is a paper cover for a letter or a card.

environment
Your **environment** is the land, water and air around you.

equal
Things that are **equal** are the same. *Mix **equal** amounts of blue and red paint.*

equipment
Equipment is a name for the things that you need to do a job. *Bowls and saucepans are types of cooking **equipment**.*

escape
escapes escaping escaped
When people or animals **escape**, they get away from somewhere. *The kitten **escaped** between Jo's legs.*

especially
Especially means more than anything else. *I **especially** liked the purple hat.*

even
1 An **even** number is a number that you reach when you count in twos. *2, 4, 6 and 8 are **even** numbers.*
■ *opposite* **odd**
2 Something that is **even** is flat or smooth. *An **even** road.*

evening
evenings
The **evening** is the part of the day between the afternoon and the night.

ever
Ever means at any time. *Have you **ever** been skating?*

every
Every means all the people or things in a group. *Marek tried **every** chocolate in the box.*

a b c d **e** f g h i j k l m n o p q r s t u v w x y z

evil

Someone who is **evil** is very bad and likes to hurt other people.

exact

Exact means just right. *Dan has the **exact** money for his bus fare.*

example

examples

An **example** is a thing that you use to show what similar things are like. *Max showed us an **example** of his drawings.*

excellent

Something that is **excellent** is very good. *An **excellent** book.*

except

Except means leaving out someone or something. *Everyone **except** Ryan enjoyed the party.*

excited

If you are **excited** about something, it makes you feel very happy and you keep thinking about it.

excuse

excuses

An **excuse** is a reason that you give for doing or for not doing something. *Lisa is often late for school, but she always has an **excuse**.*

exercise

exercises

1 You do **exercise** to keep you fit and strong. Running and swimming are kinds of exercise.
2 An **exercise** is a short piece of work that helps you to practice something you have learned. *A math **exercise**.*

exit

exits

An **exit** is a way out of a place.
■ *opposite* **entrance**

expect

expects expecting expected

If you **expect** something, you think that it will happen.

expensive

Something that is **expensive** costs a lot of money.
■ *opposite* **cheap**

experiment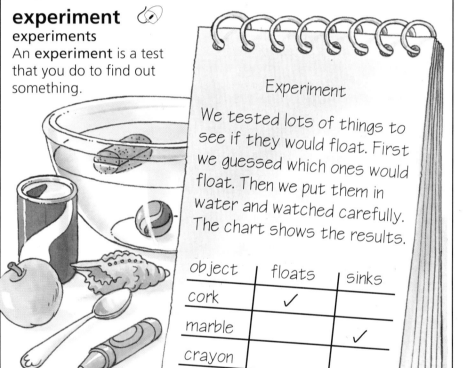

experiments

An **experiment** is a test that you do to find out something.

Experiment

We tested lots of things to see if they would float. First we guessed which ones would float. Then we put them in water and watched carefully. The chart shows the results.

object	floats	sinks
cork	✓	
marble		✓
crayon		

explain

explains explaining explained

When you **explain** something, you talk about it clearly so that other people will understand it. *Martha **explained** to her brother how the engine worked.*

explode

explodes exploding exploded

When something **explodes**, it bursts apart with a very loud noise.

explore

explores exploring explored

If you **explore** a place, you look around it for the first time. *The girls **explored** the old house.*

extinct

If a plant or an animal is **extinct**, there are no more of them alive. *Dodos are **extinct**.*

extra

Extra means more than the usual amount. *Jan made an **extra** cake.*

extraordinary

Something that is **extraordinary** is very unusual.

eye

eyes

Your **eyes** are the parts of your body that you use to see.

Ff

face
faces
Your **face** is the front part of your head.

face

forehead

eye

cheek

nose

mouth

chin

face
faces facing faced
If you **face** something, you look toward it. *Turn to face the wall.*

fact
facts
A **fact** is something that is true.

factory
factories
A **factory** is a place where things are made by machines or people. *Cars are made in factories.*

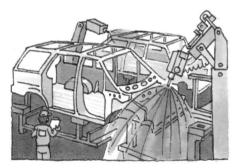

fade
fades fading faded
When a color **fades**, it gets paler. *My red shirt has faded to pink.*

fail
fails failing failed
If you **fail** at something, you do not succeed in doing it. *Jaime searched for his watch, but failed to find it.*

faint
fainter faintest
If a noise or a color is **faint**, it is not very strong. *The baby bird made a faint sound.*

fair
fairs
A **fair** is a place where people go to have fun. At fairs, people show and sell things that they have made. Most fairs have rides and games.

fair
fairer fairest
1 If something is **fair**, it seems right. *If I have a ride, it is fair that you should have one too.*
2 **Fair** hair is pale yellow.

fairy
fairies
In stories, a **fairy** is a tiny person with wings. Fairies can make magic things happen.

fall
Fall is one of the four seasons of the year. It comes between summer and winter. In the fall, the weather begins to get cold and leaves fall from the trees.

fall
falls falling fell fallen
When someone or something **falls**, they go down to the ground. *Bud fell off the ladder. The leaves fell from the trees.*

false
falser falsest
Something that is **false** is not real or not true.

family
families
A **family** is a group of people who are related. Families are usually made up of parents and children.

famous
If someone or something is **famous**, lots of people know about them.

fan
fans
A **fan** pushes air onto you so that you keep cool. Fans can work by electricity, or you can wave them with your hand.

fancy
fancier fanciest
If something is **fancy**, it is very special. Fancy things often have lots of decoration. *Is this dress too fancy to wear to school?*

fang
fangs
A **fang** is a long, pointed tooth. *Wolves have fangs.*

far
farther farthest
Far means a long way. *My friend has moved far away.*
■ *opposite* **near**

fare
fares
A **fare** is the money that you pay to travel on a bus or in a taxi.

farm
farms
A **farm** is an area of land where farmers grow crops and keep animals.

fast
faster fastest
Something that is **fast** can move quickly. *A fast car.*
　opposite **slow**

Some other words for fast are **quick, swift, rapid** and **speedy.**

fasten
fastens fastening fastened
When you **fasten** something, you close it up. *Jenny fastened her jacket. Julio fastened his seat belt.*

fat
fatter fattest
A person or an animal that is **fat** has a big, round body. *Our cat is very fat because he eats so much.*
■ opposite **thin**

father
fathers
A **father** is a man who has a child.

fault
If something bad is your **fault**, you made it happen. *It's Carter's fault that we're late because he walks so slowly.*

faucet
faucets
A **faucet** is something that you turn to make water run or stop. Sinks and bathtubs have faucets.

favorite
Your **favorite** thing is the one you like most of all. *Polly is wearing her favorite hat.*

fear
Fear is the feeling that you have when you think that something bad might happen.

feast
feasts
A **feast** is a large and special meal made for lots of people.

feather

feathers
Feathers cover a bird's body and keep it warm. They are very soft and light.

feed
feeds feeding fed
When you **feed** a person or an animal, you give them food. *Juanita never forgets to feed her cat.*

feel
feels feeling felt
1 When you **feel** something, you touch it to find out more about it. *Feel how cold my hands are!*
2 If you **feel** happy or sad, warm or cold, that is how you are at the time. *Michelle felt upset when Pedro left.*

feeling
feelings
A **feeling** tells you how you are or what mood you are in. *Todd had a sudden feeling of fear.*

fell
Fell comes from the word **fall**. *Joe often falls when he climbs trees. He fell last year and broke his leg.*

felt
Felt is a thick, soft cloth.

felt
Felt comes from the word **feel**. *I feel all right today, but yesterday I felt terrible.*

female
A **female** person or animal belongs to the sex that can have babies.

fence
fences
A **fence** is a wall made from wood or wire.

ferry
ferries
A **ferry** is a boat that takes people and cars across water.
● *See **boats** on page 16.*

festival
festivals
A **festival** is a special day or a special time of the year.

fetch
fetches fetching fetched
When dogs **fetch** something, they go to get it and bring it back. *Fido fetched Nancy's slippers.*

fever
If you have a **fever**, you have a high temperature because you are sick.

few
If you have a **few** of something, you do not have many.

field
fields
1 A **field** is a piece of land where farmers grow crops or keep animals.
2 A **field** is also piece of land where people play sports. *Our school has a new football field.*

fierce
fiercer fiercest
A **fierce** animal is wild and could hurt you. *A fierce tiger.*

fight
fights fighting fought
When people **fight**, they try to hurt each other. *The knights fought with swords.*

fill
fills filling filled
When you **fill** something, you put so much into it that you cannot add any more.

film
films
1 **Film** is a roll of special plastic that you put into a camera so that you can take photographs. *I need a new film for my camera.*
2 **Film** is also another word for movie.

filthy
filthier filthiest
Something that is **filthy** is very dirty. *Sam's boots are filthy.*

fin
fins
A **fin** is a thin, flat part that sticks out of a fish's body. Fins help fish to swim.

find
finds finding found
When you **find** something that you have lost, you see where it is. *Megan found her hamster under the bed.*

fine
1 When the weather is **fine**, it is dry and often sunny.
2 If you feel **fine**, you feel well and happy.

finger
fingers
Your **fingers** are the long, thin parts at the end of your hand. You have five fingers on each hand. One of these fingers is called a thumb.

finish
finishes finishing finished
When you **finish** something, you come to the end of it. *Kate quickly finished her lunch.*

fire
fires
A **fire** is very hot and bright and is made by burning something. *The firefighters tried to put out the fire.*

fire engine
fire engines
A **fire engine** is a kind of truck that carries equipment to put out fires. Firefighters travel to a fire in a fire engine.

firefighter
firefighters
A **firefighter** is someone whose job is to put out fires.

fireworks
Fireworks make loud noises and patterns of colored light. *The children squealed as the fireworks lit up the sky.*

firm
firmer firmest
Something that is **firm** does not move or change shape easily. *A firm mattress.*

first
If someone is **first**, they come before everyone else. *Abel came in first in the race.*

a b c d e **f** g h i j k l m n o p q r s t u v w x y z

first aid

First aid is the help that you give people who are hurt or ill before a doctor sees them.

fish

fish *or* fishes

A **fish** is a creature that lives in water. Fish use their gills to breathe under water.

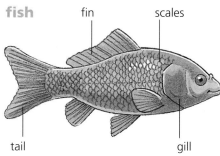

fish   fin   scales   tail   gill

fist

fists

When you make a **fist**, you close your hand tightly.

fit

fits fitting fitted

If clothes **fit** you, they are the right size for you.

fit

fitter fittest

Someone who is **fit** is healthy. *Jessie runs every day to keep fit.*

fix

fixes fixing fixed

1 If you **fix** something that is broken, you mend it so that it works again. *Luke will fix your bike so you can ride it home.*
2 If you **fix** a meal or a snack, you get it ready. *Dad fixed a delicious sandwich for me.*

fizzy

fizzier fizziest

A drink that is **fizzy** has lots of bubbles in it.

flag

flags

A **flag** is a special piece of cloth with colored shapes on it. Each country of the world has its own flag.

flame

flames

A **flame** is the hot, bright light that comes from something that is burning. *A candle flame.*

flash

flashes

A **flash** is a bright light that starts and stops suddenly. *A flash of lightning.*

flashlight

flashlights

A **flashlight** is a small light that you hold in your hand. Flashlights need batteries to make them work.

flat

flatter flattest

Something that is **flat** does not curve or have any bumps. *A flat roof. A flat lawn.*

flavor

flavors

The **flavor** of something is what it tastes like. *Which flavor of ice cream do you like best?*

fleece

Fleece is the name for the thick wool that covers a sheep or a lamb.

flew

Flew comes from the word **fly**. *I am going out to fly my new kite. Yesterday, I flew it all afternoon.*

float

floats floating floated

1 When something **floats** in water, it stays on the surface.
2 When something **floats** through the air, it moves slowly above the ground. *The balloon floated over the trees.*

flock

flocks

A **flock** is the name for a group of sheep or birds. *A flock of geese.*

flood

floods

A **flood** is a large amount of water that covers ground which is usually dry. *We had a flood in our town.*

floor

floors

1 A **floor** is the part of a room that you walk on. *On the floor was a large, red rug.*
2 A **floor** is also all the rooms on one level of a building. *Greg lives on the seventh floor.*

flour

Flour is a powder made from wheat. You use flour to make bread and cakes.

flower

flowers

A **flower** is part of a plant. Flowers are often brightly colored and some flowers smell nice.

flown

Flown comes from the word **fly**. *The baby birds are learning to fly. Some have **flown** away already.*

flu

If you have the **flu**, your body aches and you have a fever.

fly

flies

A **fly** is an insect with very thin, clear wings.

● *See* **insects** *on page 57.*

fly

flies flying flew flown

When something **flies**, it moves through the air.

foal

foals

A **foal** is a baby horse.

fog

Fog is thick cloud that is close to the ground. When there is fog, you cannot see very far.

fold

folds folding folded

When you **fold** something, you bend one part of it over another part. *Samantha **folded** the paper.*

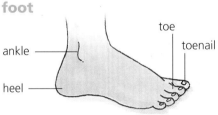

folder

folders

You keep pieces of paper in a **folder**. *A homework **folder**.*

follow

follows following followed

1 If you **follow** someone, you go behind them.

2 If something **follows** another thing, it happens after it. *Summer **follows** spring.*

fond

fonder fondest

If you are **fond** of someone, you like them very much.

> **Some words that begin** with an "f" sound, such as **photograph**, are spelled "**ph**."

food

Food is what people eat to help them stay healthy and grow. *What is your favorite food?*

foot

feet

Your **foot** is the part of your body at the end of your leg. You stand on your feet.

foot

toe
toenail
ankle
heel

football

footballs

1 **Football** is a game played by two teams on a field. One team tries to carry, throw or kick the ball down the field. The other team tries to stop them.

2 A **football** is the ball used in football games.

footprint

footprints

A **footprint** is a mark made by a foot or a shoe.

forehead

foreheads

Your **forehead** is the part of your face above your eyebrows.

foreign

Something that is **foreign** comes from another country. *Marcia collects **foreign** coins.*

forest

forests

A **forest** is a place where many trees grow close together.

forever

If something goes on **forever**, it never ends. *The story seemed to go on **forever**.*

forgave

Forgave comes from the word **forgive**. *It is kind to forgive people. Ellie **forgave** her sister for ruining her book.*

forget

forgets forgetting forgot forgotten

If you **forget** something, you do not remember it.

forgive

forgives forgiving forgave forgiven

When you **forgive** someone, you stop being angry with them.

a b c d e **f** g h i j k l m n o p q r s t u v w x y z

forgotten

Forgotten comes from the word forget. *Martin might forget to bring his book. He's **forgotten** it before.*

fork

forks

You use a **fork** to eat with. Forks have a handle and three or four sharp points.

fort

forts

A **fort** is a strong building with high walls to keep enemies out.

forward

If you move **forward**, you move ahead or toward the front. *Gary ran **forward** to catch the ball.*
■ *opposite* backward

fossil

fossils

A **fossil** is what is left of an animal or a plant that lived millions of years ago. Fossils are found in rocks.

foster

fosters fostering fostered

When people **foster** a child, the child comes to live with them for a short time and becomes part of their family.

fought

Fought comes from the word fight. *My brothers often fight. Yesterday, they **fought** over who would have the last cookie.*

found

Found comes from the word find. *Mom asked me to find my book. I **found** it under the bed.*

fountain

fountains

A **fountain** is a spray of water that is pushed up into the air.

fox

foxes

A **fox** is a wild animal that looks like a dog. Foxes have pointed ears and very thick tails.

fraction

fractions

A **fraction** is a part of a whole thing. Halves and quarters are fractions.

frame

frames

A **frame** fits around the edge of something, like a picture or a window.

freckles

Freckles are light brown spots on your skin. *Erica's nose is covered with **freckles**.*

free

1 If something is **free**, you do not have to pay any money for it. *A **free** gift.*
2 If a person or an animal is **free**, they can go where they like or do what they like.

freeze

freezes freezing froze frozen

When water **freezes**, it becomes so cold that it changes into ice. *I hope the pond will **freeze** so that we can go skating.*

freezer

freezers

A **freezer** is a machine that keeps food very cold so that it does not go bad or melt. *Linda put the ice cream in the **freezer**.*

french fry

french fries

A **french fry** is a long, thin piece of potato cooked in hot oil. French fries are often just called fries. *We had chicken and **french fries** for dinner.*

fresh

fresher freshest

1 If food is **fresh**, it has just been made or picked. *Fresh fruit.*
2 Fresh water is not salty. The water in rivers, lakes and ponds is fresh.

fried

Fried food has been cooked in hot oil or butter.

friend

friends

A **friend** is someone you like and who likes you. *Ricky and his **friend** enjoy relaxing together.*

friendly
friendlier friendliest
A **friendly** person likes to meet other people and is nice to them.

frightening
If something is **frightening**, it makes you feel afraid.
A frightening story.

Some other words for frightening are **scary**, **spooky**, **terrifying** and **petrifying**.

fringe
fringes
If clothes, curtains or cushions have a **fringe**, they have an edge made of lots of loose threads.

frog
frogs
A **frog** is a small creature with smooth skin, large eyes and strong back legs that it uses for jumping. Frogs live near water.

front
fronts
The **front** of something is the part that faces ahead or comes first. *Karen sat at the front of the bus.*
■ *opposite* **back**

frost

Frost is a thin layer of ice that covers things outside when it is very cold. *Gregory scraped the frost off the windshield.*

frown
frowns frowning frowned
When you **frown**, you push your eyebrows together and wrinkle your forehead. You frown because you are upset or because you are thinking about something.

frozen
1 If a pond is **frozen**, the surface of the water has changed into ice.

2 **Frozen** food is kept very cold so that it does not go bad.

fruit
fruits
A **fruit** is the part of a plant that holds the seeds. Many fruits are good to eat.

fry
fries frying fried
When you **fry** food, you cook it in hot oil or butter. *Dad fried an egg for his lunch.*

full
fuller fullest
If something is **full**, it cannot hold any more. *The jar is full of cookies.*
■ *opposite* **empty**

fumes
Fumes are gases that smell bad and make you cough.
Cars make fumes.

fun
When you have **fun**, you have a good time and you are happy.

funny
funnier funniest
1 If something is **funny**, it makes you laugh. *A funny joke.*
2 **Funny** also means strange or peculiar. *We heard a funny noise coming from the attic.*

fur
Fur is the soft hair that covers some animals' bodies. *Polar bears have thick, white fur.*

furious
If you are **furious**, you are very angry. *Tara was furious that her watch had been stolen.*
▲ *say* **fyoor-ee-uss**

furniture
Furniture is the name for all the big things in your home, such as tables, chairs and beds. *When we moved into our house, we bought new furniture.*

fuss
fusses fussing fussed
If you **fuss** about something, you worry about it more than you need to. *Mom is always fussing about my clothes.*

future
The **future** is the time that has not yet happened. *In the future, we might have robots to look after us.*

a b c d e **f** g h i j k l m n o p q r s t u v w x y z

Gg

gallop
gallops galloping galloped
When a horse **gallops**, it runs very fast.

game
games
1 A **game** is a sport or something that you play. Games have rules. Soccer and chess are games.

2 You also play a **game** when you pretend to be someone else. *We played a game of explorers.*

gang
gangs
A **gang** is a group of people who do things together.

gap
gaps
A **gap** is a space between two things. *Mario has a gap between his two front teeth.*

garage
garages
1 A **garage** is a building where a car is kept.
2 A **garage** is also a place where people sell gas and fix cars.

garbage
Garbage is the name for things that you throw away because you do not want them any more.

garden
gardens
A **garden** is a piece of ground where people grow flowers, plants and vegetables. *A rose garden.*

gas
gases
1 A **gas** is very light and usually cannot be seen. The air is made of gases. Some gases burn easily and are used in stoves and fireplaces.
2 Gas is also a liquid that you put in a vehicle to make it go. Gas is short for gasoline.

gate
gates
A **gate** is a kind of door in a fence, a wall or a hedge.

gave
Gave comes from the word **give**. *I want to give my dad a present. Last year, I only gave him a card.*

gentle
gentler gentlest
If you are **gentle**, you are careful and kind. *Be gentle with the baby.*

gerbil
gerbils
A **gerbil** is a small, furry animal with long back legs. Some people keep gerbils as pets.

get
got gotten
1 If you **get** something, you go and take it. *Get a shirt from the closet.*
2 **Get** also means to become. *I get hungry when I exercise.*
3 Get also means to arrive. *I got to school late.*

ghost
ghosts
A **ghost** is a person who has died who some people think they can see.

giant
giants
A **giant** is a very tall person that you read about in stories. *The giant picked up a man.*

gift
gifts
A **gift** is something special that you give to someone. *We wrapped Yasmin's gift carefully.*

giggle
giggles giggling giggled
When you **giggle**, you laugh in a silly way. *Annie kept giggling at her dad's new shorts.*

A B C D E F **G** H I J K L M N O P Q R S T U V W X Y Z

giraffe
giraffes
A **giraffe** is an animal with a very long neck and long legs. Giraffes live in herds and are the tallest animals in the world.

girl
girls
A **girl** is a female child or a young woman.

give
gives giving gave given
When you **give** something to someone, you let them have it to keep. *Ellen loves giving presents to her friends.*

glad
When you are **glad**, you are pleased and happy about something. *I'm glad that you're feeling better.*

glass
glasses
1 **Glass** is a hard material that you can see through. Windows and bottles are made of glass. It is quite easy to break glass.
2 A **glass** is a container that you drink from. Glasses are made from glass. *Dan poured some juice into his glass.*

glasses

People wear **glasses** to help them see better. Glasses have a frame that holds two special lenses in front of your eyes.

globe
globes
A **globe** is a round model of the earth. Globes are often attached to a stand so that you can spin them. *Bradley is trying to find New Zealand on his globe.*

glove
gloves
Gloves are clothes that you wear on your hands to keep them warm.

glue
Glue is a thick liquid that you use to stick things together. You use glue to make things or to mend things that are broken.

go
goes going went gone
1 **Go** means to move from one place to another. *Let's go home.*
2 **Go** also means that something will happen. *Betsy is going to be eight next week.*

goal
goals
You score a **goal** by kicking, hitting or throwing a ball into a net.

goat

goats
A **goat** is an animal with horns and a short tail. Most goats have beards.

gold
Gold is a yellow metal that is very valuable. *A gold ring.*

goldfish
goldfish
A **goldfish** is a small, orange fish. People often keep goldfish as pets.

gone
Gone comes from the word **go**. *Let's go to the park. The others have gone there already.*

good
better best
1 If something is **good**, you like it. *A good book.*
■ *opposite* **bad**

> Some other words for **good** are **marvelous**, **fantastic**, **great** and **terrific**.

2 **Good** children behave well.
■ *opposite* **bad**
3 **Good** work has been done well.
■ *opposite* **bad**

goodbye
You say **goodbye** when someone goes away.

goose
geese
A **goose** is a large bird with a long neck. Geese can swim and fly.

gotten
Gotten comes from the word **get**. *I went to get Toni a drink, but she had already gotten one.*

grab
grabs grabbing grabbed
If you **grab** something, you pick it up in a quick, rough way.

grain
grains
1 A **grain** of something, such as sand and salt, is a tiny piece of it.
2 A grain is also a seed. *A grain of rice. A grain of wheat.*

grandfather
grandfathers
Your **grandfather** is the father of your mother or your father. Children often call their grandfather grandpa or grandad.

grandmother
grandmothers
Your **grandmother** is the mother of your mother or your father. Children often call their grandmother grandma or granny.

grape
grapes
A **grape** is a small, round fruit that grows in bunches. Grapes are green or purple.

grapefruit
grapefruits
A **grapefruit** is a large, round fruit with a thick skin. Grapefruits can be yellow or pink.

grass
grasses
Grass is a plant with thin, green leaves. Grass grows in fields, parks and yards.

gravy
Gravy is a cooked sauce that you eat with meat or potatoes.

gray
Gray is the color that you make when you mix black and white. Rain clouds are gray.

graze
grazes grazing grazed
1 If you **graze** your skin, you scrape it against something. *Gary grazed his elbow on the wall.*
2 When animals **graze,** they eat the grass that is growing in a field.

great
greater greatest
1 **Great** means large. *The trees grew to a great height.*
2 **Great** also means important. *A great leader.*
3 **Great** also means very good. *We had a great holiday.*

greedy
greedier greediest
Greedy people want more of something than they need. *Gus was so greedy that he ate five bowls of ice cream.*

green
Green is the color that you make when you mix blue and yellow. Grass is green.

greenhouse
greenhouses
A **greenhouse** is a building with a glass roof and walls. People grow plants in greenhouses.

grew
Grew comes from the word **grow**. *Sunflowers grow very fast. Last week, ours grew two inches.*

griddle
griddles
You use a **griddle** to fry food. Griddles are round and flat and have a long handle.

grin
grins
A **grin** is a big smile.

grip
grips gripping gripped
If you **grip** something, you hold on to it tightly. *Sylvester gripped the baseball bat.*

ground
The **ground** is the surface that you walk on outside.

group
groups
A **group** is a number of people or things that are together or are the same in some way.

grow
grows growing
grew grown
When something
grows, it gets bigger.

growl
growls growling growled
When a dog **growls**, it makes a
long, low sound in its throat.
*Fido **growled** every time the cat
came near.*

grown
Grown comes from the word
grow. *My auntie is amazed at the
way I grow. She says I have **grown**
two inches since last summer.*

grown-up
grown-ups
A **grown-up** is someone who is
no longer a child.

grumble
grumbles grumbling grumbled
If you **grumble**, you keep on
saying that you are not happy or
that you do not like something.

guard
guards guarding guarded
If you **guard** something, you
watch it carefully to keep it safe.

guess
guesses guessing guessed
If you **guess**, you try to think of an
answer to something that you do
not know already. *Jay tried to
guess how many
pieces of candy
were in the jar.*

guest
guests
A **guest** is someone who comes to
visit you. *We have **guests** coming
to dinner tonight.*

guinea pig
guinea pigs
A **guinea pig** is a
small, furry animal
with no tail. People
often keep guinea
pigs as pets.

guitar
guitars
A **guitar** is a
musical
instrument
with strings.
You play
a guitar by
pressing the
strings with
one hand and
pulling them
with the other.

gum
gums
1 Your **gums** are the firm pink
skin around your teeth.
2 **Gum** is a kind of
candy that you
chew, but do
not swallow.

gun
guns
A **gun** is a weapon
that is used to shoot
something.

gymnastics
Gymnastics are
exercises that you do
to make you fit and
strong. *Grace
is practicing
gymnastics.*

Hh

habit
habits
A **habit** is something that you do
often, usually without thinking
about it. *Hayley's worst **habit** is
biting her nails.*

had
Had comes from the word **have**.
*We often have fish for dinner. We
had it twice last week.*

hadn't
Hadn't is a short way of saying
had not. *Danni **hadn't** seen
the film.*

hail
hails hailing
hailed
When it
hails,
small pieces
of frozen rain
fall from the
sky. *It is **hailing**
on my umbrella.*

hair
Hair is what grows on your head
and on many animals' bodies.
*Leah has very long **hair**.*

half
halves
A **half** is
one of
two pieces
that are the same
size. *Dorita cut
her apple into
halves.*

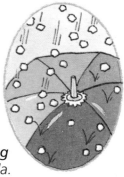

a b c d e f **g** **h** i j k l m n o p q r s t u v w x y z

hall
halls
1 A **hall** is a room with other rooms coming off it.
2 A **hall** is also a large room that is used for meetings or plays.

halo
haloes
A **halo** is a circle of light around the head of an angel.

hammer
hammers
A **hammer** is a tool that you use for hitting nails. It has a handle and a heavy metal end.
● See **tools** on page 128.

hamster
hamsters
A **hamster** is a small, furry animal that looks like a mouse. Hamsters have short tails and store food in their cheeks. They are often kept as pets.

hand
hands
Your **hand** is the part of your body at the end of your arm. You use your hands to hold things.

hand

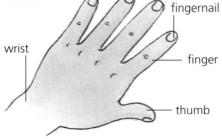

wrist

fingernail

finger

thumb

hand
hands handing handed
If you **hand** something to someone, you give it to them. *Please **hand** me a brush.*

handkerchief
handkerchiefs
A **handkerchief** is a square piece of cloth that you use to wipe your nose.

handle
handles
You use a **handle** to hold something or to move something. *The **handle** on my suitcase is broken. Josie turned the door **handle** slowly.*

handsome
Men and boys who are **handsome** are good looking.

handwriting
Your **handwriting** is the way that you write letters and words. *Sam has beautiful **handwriting**.*

hang
hangs hanging hung
If you **hang** something up, you attach the top of it to a hook or a knob. *Naomi **hung** up her coat.*

hanger
hangers
You hang your clothes on a **hanger**. Hangers can be made of plastic, metal or wood.

happen
happens happening happened
When something **happens**, it takes place. *What **happens** next?*

happy
happier happiest
When you are **happy**, you feel pleased about things.
■ opposite **sad**

> **Some other words for**
> **happy** are **glad**, **cheerful**, **pleased** and **delighted**.

harbor
harbors
A **harbor** is a safe place where boats can be tied up.

hard
harder hardest
1 Something that is **hard** is firm and solid. *A **hard** bed.*
■ opposite **soft**
2 If something is **hard**, it takes a lot of work to do it or understand it. *Math is a **hard** subject for Al.*

harmful
If something is **harmful**, it could hurt you or make you ill.

harvest
harvests
Harvest is the time when crops are cut or picked.

has
Has comes from the word **have**. *Adam will have a party for his birthday. He **has** one every year.*

hasn't

Hasn't is a short way of saying **has not**. *Micky **hasn't** arrived yet.*

hat

hats
A **hat** is something that you wear on your head.

hatch

hatches hatching hatched
When an egg **hatches**, a baby bird or animal breaks out of it.

hate

hates hating hated
If you **hate** something, you do not like it at all. *Mark **hates** cabbage.*

haunted

If a place is **haunted**, people think that there are ghosts in it.

have

has having had
1 If you **have** something, it is yours. *I **have** a new bicycle.*
2 When you **have** something, you feel it. *Luisa **has** a cold. Dale **had** a shock.*

haven't

Haven't is a short way of saying **have not**. *I **haven't** seen Kyle.*

head

heads
1 Your **head** is the part of your body where your hair, eyes, mouth and nose are. Your brain is inside your head.
2 The **head** of something is the person in charge. *The **head** of a school.*

heal

heals healing healed
When a cut **heals**, it gets better.

healthy

healthier healthiest
1 A **healthy** person is well and strong.
2 Something that is **healthy** is good for you. *I try to eat **healthy** food, such as fruit and vegetables.*

heap

heaps
A **heap** is a messy group of things. *Tyler left his clothes in a **heap** on the floor.*

hear

hears hearing heard
When you **hear**, you notice sounds with your ears.

heart

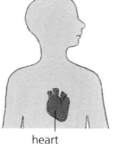

hearts
Your **heart** is the part of your body that pushes blood through your body.

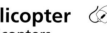
heart

heat

heats heating heated
When you **heat** something, you make it warmer. *Laura **heated** the soup in a saucepan.*

heavy

heavier heaviest
Something that is **heavy** weighs a lot. *Paul tried to lift the **heavy** suitcase.*
■ *opposite* **light**

hedge

hedges
A **hedge** is a row of bushes that make a kind of wall. You often see hedges around gardens and yards.

heel

heels
Your **heel** is the back part of your foot.

height

heights
Your **height** is how tall you are. *Courtney checked Dan's **height** to see if he had grown.*

held

Held comes from the word **hold**. *Casey offered to hold the ladder for his dad. He **held** it until his arms ached.*

helicopter

helicopters
A **helicopter** is a small aircraft without wings. It has blades on top that spin around to make it fly or hover.
● *See **aircraft** on page 7.*

he'll

He'll is a short way of saying **he will**. *Miguel is finishing his lunch. **He'll** be here soon.*

a b c d e f g **h** i j k l m n o p q r s t u v w x y z

hello
You say **hello** when you meet someone.

helmet
helmets
A **helmet** is a hard hat that you wear to protect your head. *Loretta is wearing her bicycle **helmet**.*

help
helps helping helped
If you **help** someone, you do something for them. *Kelly **helped** her dad to put up the tent.*

helpful
A **helpful** person likes to help other people.

hen
hens
A **hen** is a female chicken. Hens lay eggs.

herd
herds
A **herd** is a large group of animals. *A **herd** of elephants.*

here
Here means the place where you are. *I've lived **here** for six years.*

here's
Here's is a short way of saying **here is**. ***Here's** today's newspaper.*

herself
Herself means her and nobody else. *Emily has hurt **herself**.*

he's
He's is a short way of saying **he is**. *I'm waiting for Drew to arrive. **He's** coming at two o'clock.*

hibernate
hibernates hibernating hibernated
When animals **hibernate**, they sleep through the winter. They hibernate to stay alive when it is cold and there is not much food. Some mice and bears hibernate.

hiccup
hiccups
When you have **hiccups**, you keep making a sudden sound in your throat.

hide
hides hiding hid hidden
1 When you **hide** something, you put it where no one can see it. *Zak **hid** the present under the bed.*
2 If you **hide** your feelings, you keep them secret. *Jordan **hid** her disappointment.*

high
higher highest
1 Something that is **high** is a long way from the ground. *A **high** tower.*
2 **High** also means larger than usual. ***High** prices.*
3 A **high** voice goes up a long way. Girls and young boys have high voices when they sing.
■ *opposite* **low**

hill
hills
A **hill** is a high piece of land. Hills are not as tall as mountains.

himself
Himself means him and nobody else. *Max has hurt **himself**.*

hippopotamus
hippopotamuses
A **hippopotamus** is a large animal with short legs and thick skin. Hippopotamuses live near water.

history
History is the story of what has happened in the past.

hit
hits hitting hit
When you **hit** something, you push or knock it very hard. *Rex **hit** the ball. Peter **hit** his head.*

hobby
hobbies
A **hobby** is something that you enjoy doing in your spare time. *Jon's **hobby** is collecting pins.*

hold
holds holding held
1 If you **hold** something, you have it in your hands or your arms. *Lizzie held the kitten gently.*
2 **Hold** also means to have room for something. *This pitcher holds two pints. The room holds about 30 people.*

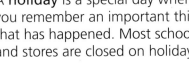

Some words that begin with an "h" sound, such as **whole**, are spelled "**wh.**"

hole
holes
A **hole** is a gap or a hollow place. *A hole in your pants. A hole in the ground.*

holiday
holidays
A **holiday** is a special day when you remember an important thing that has happened. Most schools and stores are closed on holidays.

hollow
Something that is **hollow** has an empty space inside it. *We crawled through the hollow log.*

home
homes
Your **home** is the place where you live. *We are going to stay at home today.*

homework
Homework is work that a teacher gives you to do at home.

honest
Someone who is **honest** tells the truth and can be trusted.
■ *opposite* dishonest

honey
Honey is a sweet, sticky liquid that is made by bees. You can eat honey on bread.

hood
hoods
The **hood** of a coat is the part that covers your head. *As soon as it started to rain, Toni put up her hood.*

hoof
hoofs
An animal's **hoof** is the hard part of its foot. Horses, deer and cows have hoofs.

hook
hooks
A **hook** is a curved piece of metal or plastic. Some hooks are used for hanging things up. Other hooks are used for catching things, like fish.

hop
hops hopping hopped
1 When you **hop**, you jump on one foot.
2 When birds, rabbits and kangaroos **hop**, they jump forward with their feet close together.

hope
hopes hoping hoped
If you **hope** for something, you want it to happen and think that it might. *I hope that we'll go to the circus tomorrow.*

horn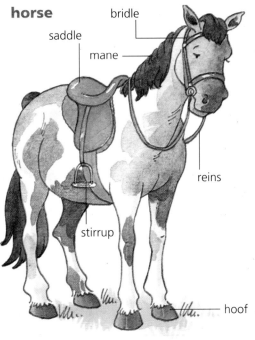
horns
1 A **horn** is one of the hard, pointed bones that grow out of some animals' heads. Goats and bulls have horns.
2 A **horn** is also a musical instrument that you blow.

horn

horrible
Something that is **horrible** is awful or frightening. *A horrible lunch. A horrible dream.*

horse
horses
A **horse** is an animal with four legs and a long tail. People ride horses.

horse

bridle
saddle
mane
reins
stirrup
hoof

hose
hoses
A **hose** is a long, narrow tube made of rubber or plastic. People use hoses to put water on gardens.

hospital
hospitals
A **hospital** is a building where people who are ill or hurt are looked after. Doctors and nurses work in hospitals.

hot
hotter hottest
Something that is **hot** has a high temperature. *A hot drink.*
■ opposite cold

hotel
hotels
A **hotel** is a big building with many bedrooms and a restaurant. People pay to stay in hotels when they are away from home.

hour
hours
An **hour** is an amount of time. An hour lasts for 60 minutes. There are 24 hours in a day.

house
houses
A **house** is a building that people live in. *Where is your house?*

hover
hovers hovering hovered
When something **hovers**, it stays in one place in the air. *The helicopter hovered over the houses.*

how
1 **How** means in what way. *How do I turn off the computer?*
2 You also use **how** when you ask about an amount. *How much money do you have? How many people are coming to the play?*

hug
hugs hugging hugged
When you **hug** someone, you hold them tightly in your arms. *Garth hugged Mario when he scored the final goal.*

huge
Something **huge** is very big. *Whales are huge.*

human being
human beings
A **human being** is a person. Men, women and children are all human beings.

hump
humps
A **hump** is a big lump. Camels have humps on their backs.

— hump

hung
Hung comes from the word **hang**. *Tim decided to hang up the picture. He hung it in his room.*

hungry
hungrier hungriest
If you are **hungry**, you want to eat something.

hunt
hunts hunting hunted
1 When animals **hunt**, they chase another animal, then kill it and eat it.
2 If you **hunt** for something, you look for it carefully. *Blake hunted everywhere for his other sock.*

hurry
hurries hurrying hurried
When you **hurry**, you do something quickly. *Georgia hurried to catch the bus.*

hurt
hurts hurting hurt
If something **hurts** you, you feel pain. *Stephanie's elbow hurt where she had hit it.*

husband
husbands
A woman's **husband** is the man she is married to.

hut
huts
A **hut** is a small house. Huts can be made from wood, mud or grass.

hutch
hutches
A **hutch** is a kind of cage made from wood and wire. People keep rabbits and other small pets in hutches.

Ii

ice

Ice is water that has frozen. Ice is very cold and hard. *The surface of the pond was covered with ice.*

iceberg
icebergs
An **iceberg** is a very large piece of ice that floats in the sea.

ice cream
Ice cream is a sweet, frozen food made from milk or cream. There are many different flavors of ice cream.

icicle
icicles
An **icicle** is a long, thin stick of ice. Icicles are made from dripping water which has frozen.

icing
Icing is used to cover cakes. It is made from sugar mixed with water or butter. Another word for icing is frosting.

I'd
1 **I'd** is a short way of saying I had. *I'd already eaten supper by the time Carlos came.*
2 **I'd** is also a short way of saying I would. *I'd love to come to your birthday party.*

idea
ideas
An **idea** is something new that you think of. *Richard had lots of ideas for a story.*

identical
If two things are **identical**, they look exactly the same. *Dana and Donna are wearing identical hats.*

ill
When you are **ill**, you are not well. Another word for ill is sick. *Chris was ill, so he had to stay in bed.*

I'll
I'll is a short way of saying I will. *I'll be home before it gets dark.*

I'm
I'm is a short way of saying I am. *I'm feeling happy today.*

imagine
imagines imagining imagined
If you **imagine** something, you have a picture of it in your mind. *Jordan imagined what it would be like to meet a dragon.*

imitate
imitates imitating imitated
If you **imitate** someone, you copy what they do.

immediately
If you do something **immediately**, you do it now. *Go to your room immediately!*

impatient
If someone feels **impatient**, they are annoyed because they have to wait. *Seth felt impatient when the bus didn't come.*

important
If something is **important**, it matters a lot. *It is important to brush your teeth twice a day.*

impossible
If something is **impossible**, it cannot be done. *It is impossible to control the weather.*

improve
improves improving improved
If something **improves**, it gets better. *My cooking has improved.*

in
1 **In** means not outside.
◼ *opposite* out
2 **In** also shows when something happens. *Sarah's birthday is in March. I'll be back in an hour.*

include
includes including included
If you **include** a person or a thing, you make them part of something. *We want to include all the children in our game.*

a b c d e f g h **i** j k l m n o p q r s t u v w x y z

increase

increases increasing increased
If something **increases**, it gets bigger.

indoors

If you are **indoors**, you are inside a building.

infectious

If a disease is **infectious**, you can catch it from another person.

information

If you ask for **information** about something, you want to know some facts about it. *Robert is looking for information about swimming classes.*

ingredient

ingredients
An **ingredient** is one of the things that goes into food. *Do you have all the ingredients you need to make a cake?*

initial

initials
An **initial** is the first letter of a word or a name. *Edward Thompson's initials are E.T.*

injured

Someone who is **injured** has been hurt.

ink

inks
Ink is a colored liquid that is used for writing or printing.

insect

insects
An **insect** is a small creature with six legs. Many insects have wings.

insects

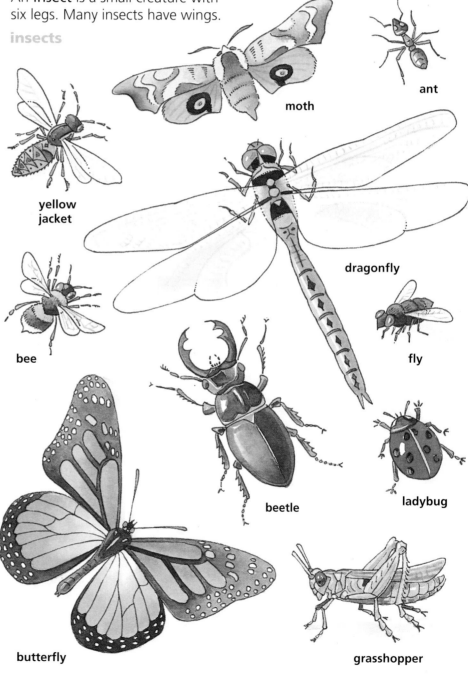

moth

ant

yellow jacket

bee

dragonfly

fly

beetle

ladybug

butterfly

grasshopper

inside

1 If something is **inside** a thing, it is in it. *A peach has a pit inside it.*
2 **Inside** also means indoors. *We went inside when it began to rain.*

instead

Instead means in place of something else. *Kyle caught the bus instead of walking home.*

A B C D E F G H I J K L M N O P Q R S T U V W X Y Z

instructions
Instructions are words and pictures that show you how to do something. *Read the instructions before you make the model.*

instrument
instruments
1 An **instrument** is something that helps you to do a job. *Doctors and dentists use instruments.*
2 An **instrument** is also something that you use to make music. *Pianos, guitars and trumpets are all instruments.*

intelligent
An **intelligent** person finds it easy to learn and to understand things.

interesting
If something is **interesting**, you want to know more about it.

interrupt
interrupts interrupting interrupted
If you **interrupt** someone, you stop them in the middle of what they are doing. *Cameron's sister interrupted him while he was listening to a tape.*

invention
inventions
An **invention** is something that nobody has made or thought of before. *My uncle has invented a machine that makes his bed.*

invisible
If something is **invisible**, you cannot see it.

invitation
invitations
When you give someone an **invitation**, you ask them to do something with you.

Ryan invites Sam
to a party on Saturday, May 4th
at Cherry Tree Cottage
Orchard Lane
from 2 o'clock to 5 o'clock
Please come dressed as a monster

iron
irons
1 **Iron** is a strong, hard metal. Gates are often made from iron.
2 People use an **iron** to make their clothes smooth. An iron has a handle and a flat metal bottom that gets hot.

irritable
If someone feels **irritable**, they are in a bad mood and are easily annoyed. *Kurt gets irritable when he hasn't had enough sleep.*

island
islands
An **island** is a piece of land with water all around it.

isn't
Isn't is a short way of saying **is not**. *Leon isn't coming today.*

itch
itches itching itched
If your skin **itches**, you want to scratch it.

its
Its means belonging to it. *The cat is playing with its ball.*

it's
1 **It's** is a short way of saying **it is**. *It's very cold today.*
2 **It's** is also a short way of saying **it has**. *It's been a long day.*

itself
Itself means it and nothing else. *This machine works by itself.*

I've
I've is a short way of saying **I have**. *I've been here before.*

Jj

jacket
jackets
A **jacket** is a short coat.

jam
jams
Jam is a thick, sweet food that is made by boiling fruit and sugar together. *Strawberry jam on toast.*

jar
jars
You use a **jar** to keep things in. Jars are usually made of glass. People buy jelly and jam in jars.

jaw
jaws
Your **jaw** is the bone at the bottom of your face. It moves when you speak or eat.

jealous
If you are **jealous**, you are upset because someone has something that you do not have. *Charlie felt jealous when Curtis got his new computer.*

jeans
Jeans are pants that are made from a strong cotton material, called denim.

jelly
jellies
Jelly is a sweet food that is made by boiling fruit juice and sugar.

> **Some words that begin** with a "j" sound, such as **gentle**, **gerbil** and **giant**, are spelled with a "g."

jet
jets
A **jet** is an aircraft that travels very fast. Jets have special engines.
● *See* **aircraft** *on page 7.*

jewel
jewels
A **jewel** is a very valuable stone. Diamonds are jewels.

jewelry
Jewelry is the name for pretty things, such as rings and pins, that you wear on your body or on your clothes.

jewelry

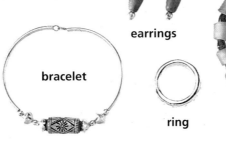

earrings

bracelet

ring

jigsaw
jigsaws
A **jigsaw** is a picture that has been cut into pieces. You make the picture again by putting the pieces together.

job
jobs
1 A **job** is the work that someone does to earn money. *Mom has a job in a bank.*
2 A **job** is also something that needs to be done. *There are lots of jobs to do in the yard.*

join
joins joining joined
1 If you **join** things, you put them together. *Kim joined the pieces of wood to make a table.*
2 If you **join** a club, you become a member of it. *Carly has joined a gymnastics club.*

joint
joints
A **joint** is a part of your body where two bones meet. Elbows and knees are joints.

pin

necklace

A B C D E F G H I J K L M N O P Q R S T U V W X Y Z

joke

jokes

A **joke** is something that you say to make people laugh.

What do you call a cat with eight legs?

What's orange and sounds like a parrot?

A carrot.

An octopuss.

What always follows a crocodile?

Its tail.

What do you find in the middle of India?

The letter "d".

journey

journeys

When you go on a **journey**, you travel from one place to another. *Annie has a long journey home.*

journal

journals

A **journal** is a book in which you write down things that happen each day. Another word for journal is diary. *Mrs Ross asked us to keep a journal of our summer vacation.*

jug

jugs

A jug is a container that holds a liquid. Jugs often have a narrow neck and a small handle.

juggle

juggles juggling juggled

When you **juggle**, you keep things in the air by throwing and catching them, one after the other. *Lee can juggle with balls and clubs.*

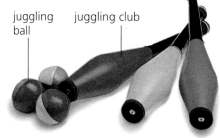

juggling ball

juggling club

juice

juices

Juice is the liquid that comes from fruit or vegetables. *Billy loves drinking apple juice.*

jump

jumps jumping jumped

When you **jump**, you bend your knees and push yourself suddenly into the air. *Leah jumped over the puddle.*

> **Some other words for** jump are **leap**, **spring** and **bound**.

jumper

jumpers

A **jumper** is a kind of dress without sleeves. Women and girls wear jumpers over blouses or sweaters.

jungle

jungles

A **jungle** is a place in a hot country where many trees and plants grow. Monkeys, parrots and snakes live in jungles.

Junior

Junior is used after the name of a boy who has the same name as his father. *Wiliam Brown Junior is the son of William Brown.*

junk

Junk is a name for things that people do not want. *Adam's room is full of junk.*

just

1 If something has **just** happened, it happened a short time ago. *Stephanie has just left.*
2 **Just** also means the right amount. *There were just enough seats for everyone.*
3 **Just** also means only. *Don't worry about the noise. It's just the wind in the trees.*

Kk

kangaroo
kangaroos
A **kangaroo** is a large animal that moves around by jumping. Female kangaroos carry their babies in a bag on their stomach, called a pouch.

Some words that begin with a "k" sound, such as **candle**, **canoe**, **carrot** and **castle**, are spelled with a "c."

keep
keeps keeping kept
1 When you **keep** something, you have it and do not give it away. *Ed keeps all his old toys.*
2 If you **keep** doing something, you do it again and again. *Kerry kept laughing at my jokes.*
3 If you **keep** a promise, you do what you said you would do.
4 **Keep** also means to make something stay the same. *Please keep the door closed.*

kennel
kennels
A **kennel** is a place where your pet can stay when you are away.

kept
Kept comes from the word **keep**. *Bradley keeps his diary under his bed. He has always kept it there.*

kettle
kettles
A **kettle** is a metal container that is used to boil water.

key
keys

1 A **key** is a piece of metal that has been cut into a special shape. You use a key to open a lock or to start a car.
2 A **key** is also one of the parts of a piano or a computer that you press to make it work.

kick
kicks kicking kicked
When you **kick** something, you hit it with your foot. *Carson kicked the soccer ball into the air.*

kid
kids
1 A **kid** is a young goat.
2 A **kid** is also a child.

kill
kills killing killed
To **kill** means to make something die. *The frost has killed most of the plants.*

kind
kinds
Things of the same **kind** are alike or belong to the same group. *A butterfly is a kind of insect.*

kind
kinder kindest
A **kind** person helps other people. *It was kind of Pat to give us tea.*

king
kings
A **king** is a man who rules a country. Kings come from royal families and are not chosen by the people.

kiss
kisses kissing kissed
When you **kiss** someone, you touch them with your lips.

kitchen
kitchens
A **kitchen** is a room where you cook meals.

kite
kites
A **kite** is a frame covered with paper or cloth with a very long string attached to it. You can fly a kite in the wind.

kitten
kittens
A **kitten** is a very young cat.

A B C D E F G H I J **K** L M N O P Q R S T U V W X Y Z

knee
knees
Your **knee** is the joint in the middle of your leg, where it bends.

kneel
kneels kneeling knelt
When you **kneel**, you get down on your knees.

knew
Knew comes from the word **know**. *Carrie didn't know about the party, but she knew that we were planning something.*

knife
knives
A **knife** is a tool that you use to cut things. Knives have a handle and a metal blade.

knight
knights
A **knight** was a soldier who lived hundreds of years ago. Knights wore armor and fought for their king.

knit
knits
knitting
knitted
When you **knit**, you make clothes from yarn, using two long needles. *Meg is knitting a scarf.*

knob
knobs
A **knob** is a round handle on a door or a drawer.

knock
knocks
knocking
knocked
1 If you **knock** on something, you hit it. *I knocked on the door until someone heard me.*
2 If you **knock** something over, you make it fall. *Terri has knocked over a glass of milk.*

knot
knots
A **knot** is a place where something, such as string, is tied. *Tie a knot in the string to make the package safe.*

knot

know
knows knowing knew known
1 If you **know** something, you have it in your mind. *Sally knows the answers to all the teacher's questions.*
2 If you **know** someone, you have met them before. *I have known Adam for years.*

Ll

label
labels
A **label** is a piece of paper or cloth that is attached to something. Clothes often have labels that tell you how to wash them.

lace
Lace is a thin material with lots of holes in it. It is sometimes used to decorate clothes.

laces
Laces are like long pieces of string. You use laces to tie up your shoes.

ladder
ladders
A **ladder** is a set of steps that can be moved around. *Dad used a ladder to climb up to the roof.*

lady
ladies
A **lady** is a woman.

ladybug
ladybugs
A **ladybug** is a red or yellow insect with black spots.
See **insects** on page 57.

laid
Laid comes from the word **lay**. *I asked Pedro to lay the clothes on the chair, but he laid them on the bed.*

a b c d e f g h i j **k l** m n o p q r s t u v w x y z

lake

lakes
A **lake** is a large area of water with land all around it.

lamb

lambs
A **lamb** is a young sheep.

lamp

lamps
A **lamp** makes light. Most lamps work by electricity. *Jenny has a lamp on her desk.*

land

Land is the name for the parts of the earth that are not covered by water. *We traveled by land.*

land

lands landing landed
When a plane **lands**, it comes down from the air to the ground.

landing

landings
A **landing** is the area of a house at the top of the stairs. A landing leads to other rooms.

lane

lanes
1 A **lane** is a narrow road, usually in the country.
2 A **lane** is also one of the strips that a wide road is divided into. Freeways usually have three lanes on each side.

language

languages
Language is a name for the words that people use to speak and write to each other. *Fritz can speak three languages.*

lantern

lanterns
A **lantern** is a lamp that you carry. Lanterns sometimes have a candle inside them.

lap

laps
Your **lap** is the top part of your legs, when you are sitting down. *The kitten sat on Robyn's lap.*

lap

laps lapping lapped
When an animal **laps** up a drink, it uses its tongue to drink.

large

larger largest
If something is **large** it takes up a lot of space. *A large room. A large bag of popcorn.*

last

1 Something that is **last** comes at the end. *Z is the last letter of the alphabet.*
2 **Last** also means the time before this. *I saw Patrick last week.*

late

later latest
1 If you are **late**, you arrive after the right time. *Kenny was late because his watch was wrong.*
2 **Late** also means near the end of something. *We arrived home late in the evening.*
■ *opposite* **early**

laugh

laughs laughing laughed
When you **laugh**, you make sounds which show that you think that something is funny. *Laura always laughs at Carl's jokes.*

law

laws
A **law** is a rule that everyone in a state or a country must obey.

lawn

lawns
A **lawn** is a large area of cut grass. You see lawns in parks and around people's houses.

lay

lays laying laid
1 If you **lay** something somewhere, you put it down carefully. *Tony laid the spoons on the table.*

2 When a bird **lays** an egg, the egg comes out of its body.

lay

Lay comes from the word **lie**. *Georgia decided to lie on the sofa. She lay there for hours.*

layer

layers
A **layer** is something flat that lies above or below something else. *My birthday cake has three layers.*

lazy

lazier laziest
Someone who is **lazy** does not want to do any work. *Zack is too lazy to do his homework.*

A B C D E F G H I J K L M N O P Q R S T U V W X Y Z

lead
leads
The **lead** in a pencil is the black part that makes a mark.
▲ *rhymes with head*

lead
leads leading led
1 If you **lead** someone to a place, you go with them to show them where it is. *Maddy led us to the station.*
2 If you **lead** a group of people, you are in charge of them.
▲ *rhymes with seed*

leaf
leaves
A **leaf** is one of the thin, flat parts of a plant or a tree. Leaves are usually green but some leaves change color in the fall.

leak
leaks leaking leaked
If a container **leaks**, the liquid inside it comes out slowly through a small hole. *This pail is leaking.*

lean
leans leaning leaned
If something **leans**, it bends to one side. *Look at the way that tower is leaning!*

leap
leaps leaping leaped
When you **leap**, you jump up in the air or jump over something. *Marek leaped over the puddle.*

learn
learns learning learned
When you **learn** something, you get to know it or understand it. *Juanita is learning to play the clarinet.*

leash
leashes
A **leash** is a long strip of leather or a chain that you attach to a dog's collar. You use the leash to control the dog.

least
Least means the smallest amount. *Nobody ate much, but Max ate the least.*
■ *opposite* **most**

leather
Leather is made from animal skin. It is used to make shoes and bags.

leave
leaves leaving left
1 If you **leave** a place, you go away from it.
2 When you **leave** something in a place, you let it stay where it is.

led
Led comes from the word **lead**. *Rod will lead us up the mountain. He has led us before.*

left
You have a **left** hand and a right hand. Most people draw with their right hand, but some people use their left hand.
■ *opposite* **right**

left

left
Left comes from the word **leave**. *We promised to leave early, so we left straight after lunch.*

leg
legs
1 Your **legs** are the parts of your body that you use for standing and walking.
2 The **legs** on a table or a chair are the parts that hold it up.

lemon
lemons
A **lemon** is a yellow fruit with a thick skin. Lemons are juicy and have a sour taste.

lend
lends lending lent
If you **lend** something to someone, you let them have it for a short time. *I lent Mack my pen.*

length
lengths
The **length** of something is how long it is. *Dad measured the length of the wood.*

lens
lenses
A **lens** is a special, curved piece of glass or plastic. Lenses are used in glasses and telescopes to make things look clearer or bigger.

a b c d e f g h i j k l m n o p q r s t u v w x y z

lent

Lent comes from the word **lend**. *Bobby often lends me his bike. He lent it to me yesterday.*

leopard

leopards

A **leopard** is a large wild cat. Leopards have dark yellow fur with black spots.

▲ *say **lep**-erd*

leotard

leotards

A **leotard** is a piece of clothing that fits tightly. You can wear a leotard when you dance or do exercise. *Courtney wears a leotard for her ballet class.*

▲ *say **lee**-oh-tard*

less

Less means not as much. *I had less to eat than my brother.*

■ *opposite* **more**

lesson

lessons

A **lesson** is a period of time when you are taught something. *A swimming lesson.*

let

lets letting let

If someone **lets** you do something, they say that you can do it. *Dad let us stay up late.*

let's

Let's is a short way of saying let us. *Let's go to the movies.*

letter

letters

1 A **letter** is a sign that you use to write words. A, M and Z are letters.

2 A **letter** is also a message that you write on paper. You usually put letters in envelopes to mail them.

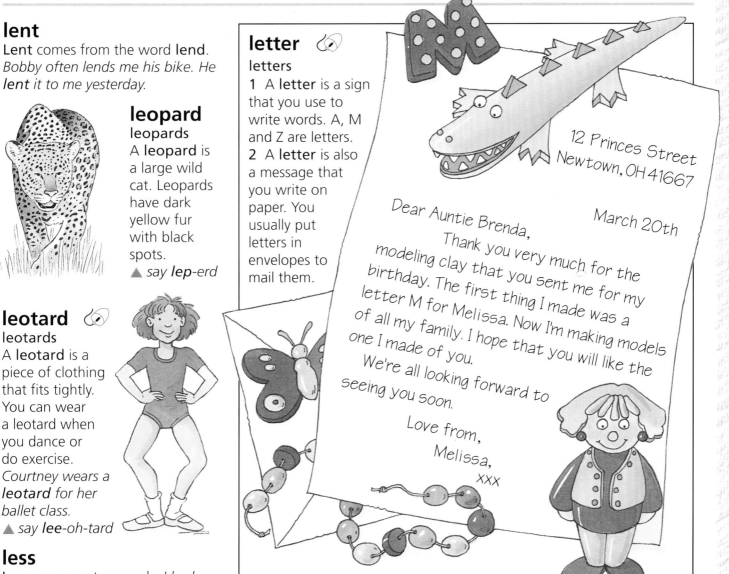

12 Princes Street
Newtown, OH 41667

March 20th

Dear Auntie Brenda,
Thank you very much for the modeling clay that you sent me for my birthday. The first thing I made was a letter M for Melissa. Now I'm making models of all my family. I hope that you will like the one I made of you. We're all looking forward to seeing you soon.

Love from,
Melissa,
xxx

lettuce

lettuces

A **lettuce** is a vegetable with large leaves that are usually green. You use lettuce to make salads.

level

levels

A **level** is a particular height. *Hang the pictures on the wall at eye level.*

level

Something that is **level** is flat and smooth. *Football fields must always be level.*

library

libraries

A **library** is a place where a lot of books are kept. You can borrow books from a library to read at home.

lick

licks licking licked

If you **lick** something, you move your tongue along it. *Leila licked her lollipop.*

lid
lids

A **lid** is the top of a box or other container. To open the container, you lift up the lid or take it off.

lie
lies lying lied

If you **lie**, you say something that is not true.

lie
lies lying lay lain

When you **lie** down, you rest with your body flat on a bed or another surface.

life
lives

Life is the time that someone is alive. *My grandfather had a long and interesting life.*

lifeguard
lifeguards

A **lifeguard** is someone who watches over swimmers to make sure that they are safe.

lift
lifts lifting lifted

If you **lift** something, you pick it up. *Jonathan lifted the kitten out of the basket.*

light
lights

1 When there is **light**, you can see things. The sun, lamps and flashlights make light.
2 A **light** is something, such as a lamp, that gives out light.

light
lights lighting lit

When you **light** a fire, you make it burn. *Mom lit a campfire.*

light
lighter lightest

1 If it is **light**, you can see things.
■ *opposite* **dark**
2 **Light** colors are pale.
■ *opposite* **dark**
3 Something that is **light** does not weigh very much.
■ *opposite* **heavy**

lighthouse
lighthouses

A **lighthouse** is a tower with a flashing light on top of it. Lighthouses warn ships of danger.

lightning
Lightning is a sudden flash of light in the sky. You sometimes see lightning when there is a storm.

like
likes liking liked

When you **like** something, you enjoy it and think that it is good.

like
If two things are **like** each other, they are the same in some way.

line
lines

1 A **line** is a long, thin mark. *My writing paper has lines printed on it.*
2 A **line** is also a number of people or things in a row. *We stood in a line for the team photograph.*

lion
lions

A **lion** is a large wild cat with light brown fur. Lions live in Africa and India.

lip
lips

Your **lips** are the edges of your mouth.

liquid
liquids

A **liquid** is something that can be poured. Water, oil and fruit juice are all liquids.

list
lists

A **list** is a group of things that are written down one after the other. *A shopping list.*

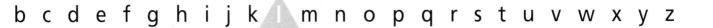

a b c d e f g h i j k **l** m n o p q r s t u v w x y z

listen

listens listening listened
When you **listen**, you pay attention to what you are hearing. *Mrs. Ross asked everybody to listen carefully.*

lit

Lit comes from the word **light**. *Dad decided to light a fire. He lit it a long way from the house.*

litter

1 **Litter** is garbage that has been dropped outside. *The streets were dirty and full of litter.*
2 A **litter** is a group of baby animals born at the same time to the same mother. *A litter of puppies.*

little

1 If something is **little**, it is small.
2 **Little** also means not much. *Mario eats very little.*

live

lives living lived
1 Something that **lives** is alive.
2 If you **live** somewhere, your home is there. *Jan lives in Chicago.*

lively

livelier liveliest
Someone who is **lively** has a lot of energy. *Emily is a lively dancer.*

lizard

lizards
A **lizard** is a small reptile with a long body and a tail. Lizards lay eggs.

load

loads
A **load** is something heavy that has to be moved. *The truck took a load of sand to the house.*

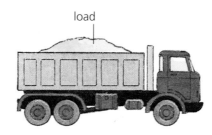
load

loaf

loaves
A **loaf** is bread that has been baked in a shape.

lobster

lobsters
A **lobster** is a sea creature with a shell and ten legs. You can eat lobsters. Lobsters turn pink when you cook them.
● *See* **sea creatures** *on page 104.*

lock

locks
A **lock** keeps things such as doors and cupboards shut. You need a key to open a lock. *My diary has a lock on it.*

log

logs
A **log** is a thick piece of wood that has been cut from a tree.

lollipop

lollipops
A **lollipop** is a large candy on a stick.

lonely

lonelier loneliest
If you are **lonely**, you feel unhappy because you are alone.

long

longer longest
1 If something is **long**, one of its ends is far away from the other. *Kamala has very long hair.*
2 If something takes a **long** time, it takes a lot of time.
■ *opposite* **short**

look

looks looking looked
1 When you **look** at something, you use your eyes to see it. *Lauren is looking at the view.*
2 If you **look** for something, you try to find it. *Sylvester looked everywhere for his hamster.*
3 The way you look is the way that people see you. *Shane looks happy today.*

loop

loops
A **loop** is a circle made with a rope, a string or a ribbon. *A bow has two loops.*

loose

looser loosest
1 Clothes that are **loose** do not fit closely. *These jeans are too loose for me.*
2 Something that is **loose** is not attached firmly. *The handle on this suitcase is loose.*

lose
loses losing lost
1 If you **lose** something, you do not know where it is. *Jamie has lost his watch.*
2 If you **lose** a game or a race, you do not win it.

lot
A **lot** is a large amount. *I had a lot of birthday cards.*

loud
louder loudest
Something that is **loud** makes a lot of noise. *Mom doesn't like loud music.*
■ *opposite* **quiet**

lounge
lounges
A **lounge** is a room where you can sit and relax. Airports and hospitals have lounges.

love
loves loving loved
If you **love** someone, you like them very much.

lovely
lovelier loveliest
If something is **lovely**, you really enjoy looking at it.

low
lower lowest
1 Something that is **low** is not far from the ground. *A low chair.*
2 **Low** also means smaller than usual. *Low prices. A low temperature.*
3 A **low** voice goes down a long way. Most men have low voices.
■ *opposite* **high**

lucky
luckier luckiest
If you are **lucky**, good things happen to you that you have not planned.

luggage
Luggage is the name for the suitcases and bags that you take with you when you travel.

lump
lumps
1 A **lump** is a piece of something. *Pick up that lump of coal.*
2 A **lump** is also something round that sticks out. *My gravy has lumps in it. Look at the lump on my head!*

lunch
lunches
Lunch is the meal that you eat in the middle of the day. *Francesca takes her lunch to school in a lunchbox.*

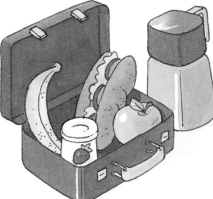

lying
Lying comes from the word **lie**. *Mom told me never to lie. She was very angry when she heard me lying to Tyler.*

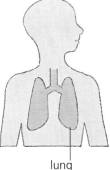

lung
lungs
Your **lungs** are inside your chest. When you breathe, air goes in and out of your lungs.

lung

Mm

machine
machines
A **machine** is something that does a job. Machines have many moving parts. Cars, computers and cranes are all machines.

mad
madder maddest
If you are **mad**, you feel angry.

made
Made comes from the word **make**. *Amy makes excellent cakes. Yesterday, she made a fruit cake.*

magic
1 In stories, **magic** is the power to make impossible things happen. *By magic, the stone became gold.*
2 **Magic** is also a name for clever tricks that look impossible.

magician
magicians
1 In stories, a **magician** is someone who uses magic to do impossible things.
2 A **magician** is also someone who does surprising tricks.

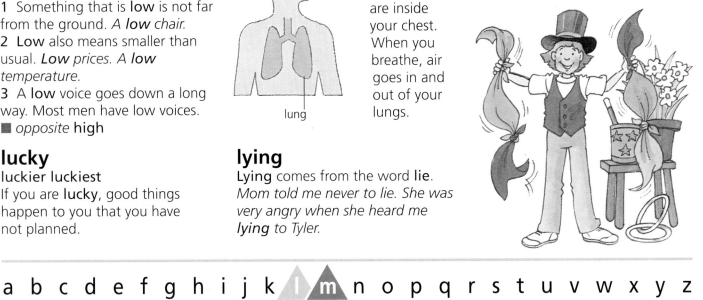

magnet
magnets
A **magnet** is a special piece of metal that makes other metals stick to it. Things that are made of iron and steel stick to magnets.

magnifying glass
magnifying glasses A **magnifying glass** is a glass lens that makes things look bigger.

mail
Mail is a name for the letters and packages that people send.

mail
mails mailing mailed
If you **mail** a letter or a package, you put it in a mailbox to be sent to someone.

main
Main means the biggest or the most important. *The main entrance to the station. The main meal of the day.*

make
makes making made
1 If you **make** something, you put it together. *Jo made a model.*
2 If you **make** something happen, it happens because of what you do. *Stacey teased her brother and made him cry.*

male
A **male** person or animal belongs to the sex that cannot have babies.

mammal
mammals
A **mammal** is an animal that has babies and can feed them with its own milk. Human beings, whales and dogs are all mammals.

man
men
A **man** is an adult, male human being.

manage
manages managing managed
If you **manage** to do something, you do it even though it is difficult. *Patsy managed to swim 20 lengths of the pool.*

manners
Your **manners** are the way that you behave. *Gregory has very good manners. He is always polite and helpful.*

many
Many means a large number. *There are many flowers in our garden.*

map
maps
A **map** is a drawing that shows you where places are. Maps can show roads, rivers and buildings.

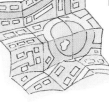

marble
marbles
1 A **marble** is a small, glass ball that is used to play a game called marbles.
2 Marble is a hard rock. Statues and buildings can be made from marble.

march
marches marching marched
When soldiers **march**, they all walk together with steps of the same size.

margarine
Margarine is a soft, yellow food like butter. You can spread margarine on bread or use it for cooking.

margin
margins
A **margin** is a long, blank space along the edge of a page.

mark
marks
1 A **mark** is a dirty spot or a stain on something.
2 Teachers give you a **mark** to show how good or bad your work is.

market
markets
A **market** is a place where you can buy things. Markets are often held outdoors.

marmalade
Marmalade is a sweet, sticky food made from oranges or lemons. People eat marmalade on toast for breakfast.

marry
marries marrying married
When a man and a woman **marry**, they promise to spend their lives together.

A B C D E F G H I J K L **M** N O P Q R S T U V W X Y Z

marsh

marshes

A **marsh** is an area of wet and muddy land. Many birds and animals live on marshes.

mask

masks

A **mask** is something that you wear to cover your face. When you dress up in a costume, you often wear a mask.

mat

mats

1 A **mat** is a small piece of carpet or other material that is used to cover part of a floor.
2 A **mat** is also a small piece of cloth or other material that you put on a table to protect it.

match

matches

1 A **match** is a short, thin stick of wood with a special tip. It produces a flame when you rub its tip on a rough surface.
2 A **match** is a game played by two players or two teams. *A tennis match.*

match

matches matching matched

If two or more things **match**, they look the same in some way. *Jessica's hat, scarf and gloves all match. They are all exactly the same color.*

material

materials

1 **Material** is a name for anything used to make something else. Bricks, wood and glass are all building materials.
2 **Material** is also a name for wool, cotton and other kinds of cloth. *Kayla's dress is made from thick material.*

math

When you study **math**, you learn about numbers, amounts and shapes.

matter

matters mattering mattered

If something **matters** to you, you care a lot about it and think that it is important. *It matters to me that you come to my party.*

mattress

mattresses

A **mattress** is the thick, soft part of a bed that you lie on. Mattresses often have springs inside them.

may

might

1 If something **may** happen, there is a chance that it will happen. *Susie may visit me today.*
2 If you **may** do something, you are allowed to do it. *Anna says I may use her computer.*

meadow

meadows

A **meadow** is a field of grass.
▲ *say med-oh*

meal

meals

A **meal** is the food that you eat at certain times of the day. Breakfast, lunch and dinner are meals.

mean

means meaning meant

1 When you say what something **means**, you explain it. *Casey told us what the signs meant.*
2 If you **mean** to do something, you plan to do it. *I didn't mean to hurt my brother.*

mean

meaner meanest

A **mean** person is not kind. *It was mean of Carl to tease you.*

measles

Measles is an infectious disease. When you have measles, lots of red spots appear on your skin and you have a high temperature.

measure

measures measuring measured

When you **measure** something, you find out how big or how heavy it is.

meat

Meat is a kind of food that comes from animals. Beef, lamb and chicken are types of meat.

a b c d e f g h i j k l **m** n o p q r s t u v w x y z

medal
medals
Medals are given to people as prizes or rewards. A medal often looks like a coin hanging from a ribbon.

medicine

medicines
Medicine is something that people take if they are sick to make them well again.

medium
Medium means between big and small in size.

meet
meets meeting met
If you **meet** someone, you both go to the same place at the same time. *I **met** Candy outside the museum.*

melt
melts melting melted
When something **melts**, it becomes much warmer and changes into liquid. *My ice cream has melted.*

member
members
If you are a **member** of a group, you are one of the people in it.

memory
You use your **memory** to remember things. If you have a good memory, you remember things. If you have a bad memory, you forget them.

mend
mends mending mended
When you **mend** something that is damaged or broken, you work on it so that it can be used again. *Mom has mended my jeans.*

mention
mentions mentioning mentioned
If you **mention** something, you talk about it for a short time. *Eugene **mentioned** that it was time to leave.*

menu
menus
A **menu** is a list of food that you can buy in a restaurant or a café.

mess
If something is a **mess**, it is very untidy and sometimes dirty. *Dad told me to clean up the mess in my room.*

mermaid
mermaids
In stories, a **mermaid** is a magical creature that lives in the ocean. Mermaids have the face, chest and arms of a girl and the tail of a fish. A male mermaid is called a merman.

message
messages
A **message** is a piece of information that you send to someone or leave for someone.

Don't forget your lunch!

met
Met comes from the word **meet**. *The members of the computer club meet every week. Last term, they **met** on Fridays.*

metal
metals
A **metal** is a hard material that is found in the ground. Metals are used to make things such as machines, vehicles and jewelry. Iron, copper and gold are metals.

microphone
microphones
You use a **microphone** to make your voice sound louder.

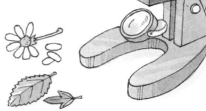

microscope
microscopes
A **microscope** makes small things look much bigger, so that you can see and study them. *We looked at leaves and petals through a microscope.*

midday
Midday is the middle of the day. *We usually eat our lunch at midday.*

middle
1 The **middle** of something is the place that is the same distance away from all its sides. *There's a tree in the **middle** of our yard.*
2 If you are in the **middle** of something, you have started it and want to finish it. *Jordan is in the **middle** of watching her favorite TV program.*

midnight
Midnight is 12 o'clock at night.

might
Might comes from the word **may**. *We may go out today. Sarah said she **might** come too.*

milk
Milk is a white liquid that mothers feed to their babies. People often drink cows' milk.

mime
mimes
miming
mimed
When you **mime**, you act without using any words. *Ella **mimed** being trapped in a tower.*

mind
minds
Your **mind** is the part of you that thinks, remembers and imagines.

mine
mines
A **mine** is a place where things, such as coal or diamonds, are dug out of the ground.

mine
If something is **mine**, it belongs to me. *Don't touch that chocolate. It's **mine**!*

minus
Minus means take away. The sign for minus is - . *Ten **minus** four is six.*

minute
minutes
A **minute** is an amount of time. A minute lasts for 60 seconds. There are 60 minutes in an hour.

mirror
mirrors
A **mirror** is a special piece of glass that you can see yourself in. *Nat is looking at himself in the **mirror**.*

mischievous
Someone who is **mischievous** is lively and naughty. *The **mischievous** children helped themselves to the cake.*

miserable
Someone who is **miserable** feels sad and unhappy. *Robin is **miserable** because it is raining.*

miss
misses missing missed
1 If you **miss** someone, you are unhappy because they are not with you.
2 If you **miss** a train or a bus, you do not manage to catch it.
3 If you **miss** a ball, you do not manage to catch it or hit it.

mist
Mist is cloud that is close to the ground. When there is a mist, you cannot see very far.

mistake
mistakes
If you make a **mistake**, you do something wrong.

mix
mixes mixing mixed
When you **mix** things, you put them together to make one thing. *Joel **mixed** red and yellow paint to make orange paint.*

mixture
mixtures
A **mixture** is something that you make by mixing things together. Mud is a mixture of earth and water.

moan
moans moaning moaned
1 If you **moan**, you make a long, low sound because you are unhappy or hurt. *The wounded soldier **moaned** softly.*
2 If you **moan** about something, you say you are unhappy about it. *Ross **moaned** about his homework.*

model
models
A **model** is a small copy of something. *Jake has a **model** of a sailboat inside a bottle.*

mom
moms
Mom is a name for your mother.

moment
moments
A **moment** is a very short amount of time. *Wait a **moment**.*

money
You use **money** to buy things.

a b c d e f g h i j k l **m** n o p q r s t u v w x y z

monkey

monkeys

A **monkey** is an animal with long arms and legs, a very long tail and a furry body. Monkeys live in trees in hot countries.

monster

monsters

In stories, a **monster** is a large, fierce animal or person. Monsters often look very ugly.

month

months

A **month** is a period of about four weeks. There are twelve months in a year. *May and July are* ***months***.

mood

moods

Your **mood** is the way that you feel. *Toni is in a good* ***mood*** *because she is on vacation.*

moon

The **moon** is the large, bright object that you see in the sky at night. It takes one month for the moon to travel around the earth.

more

More means larger in number or size. *My brother ate* ***more*** *lunch than I did.*

■ *opposite* less

morning

mornings

The **morning** is the part of the day before noon.

most

Most means the largest amount. *My brother ate more than I did, but my father ate* ***most*** *of all.*

moth

moths

A **moth** is an insect with four large wings.

● See **insects** *on page 57.*

mother

mothers

A **mother** is a woman who has a child.

motorcycle

motorcycles

A **motorcycle** is a large, heavy bicycle with an engine.

motorcycle　　passenger seat

rider's seat

fuel tank

handlebars　　headlight

fender

exhaust pipe　　engine

motorist

motorists

A **motorist** is someone who drives a car or who is a passenger in a car.

mountain

mountains

A **mountain** is a very high piece of land. Mountains are higher than hills.

mouse

mice

1 A **mouse** is a small, furry animal with a long tail and sharp teeth. *The* ***mice*** *chased each other through the field.*
2 A **mouse** is also something that you use to move things on a computer screen.

mouth

mouths

Your **mouth** is the part of your face that you use to eat and talk.

move

moves moving moved

1 When things **move**, they change position and do not stay still. *The leaves moved gently.*
2 When people **move**, they go from one place to another. *Meg moved to a different chair.*

movie

movies

When you watch a **movie**, you see moving pictures on a screen. *We watched a movie on TV.*

much
Much means a large amount.
Fran doesn't eat **much***.*

mud
Mud is dirt that is wet and sticky.

mug
mugs
A **mug** is a large cup with straight sides.

multiply
multiplies multiplying multiplied
When you **multiply** numbers, you add the same number to itself several times.

$$4 \times 3 = 12$$

munch
munches munching munched
When you **munch** your food, you bite or chew it in a noisy way.

muscle
muscles
A **muscle** is a part of your body. Muscles are attached to bones and pull on them to make them move.

museum
museums
A **museum** is a place where you can see interesting things.

mushroom
mushrooms
A **mushroom** is a plant that looks like an umbrella. You can eat some mushrooms.

music
Music is a pattern of sounds. People make music by playing musical instruments or by singing.

musical instrument
musical instruments
A **musical instrument** is something that you use to make music. You can play musical instruments by blowing into them or hitting them, or by pulling their strings.

musical instruments

violin and bow

guitar

cello

flute

harmonica

clarinet

trumpet

saxophone

must
If you **must** do something, you have to do it. *I* **must** *go now.*

mustn't
Mustn't is a short way of saying must not. *You* **mustn't** *go home yet.*

a b c d e f g h i j k l **m** n o p q r s t u v w x y z

myself
Myself means me and nobody else. *I have hurt myself.*

mysterious
Something that is **mysterious** is difficult to understand or explain. *We heard a mysterious sound.*

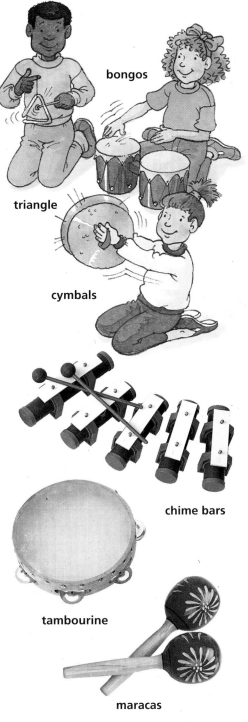

bongos

triangle

cymbals

chime bars

tambourine

maracas

Nn

nag
nags nagging nagged
If someone **nags** you, they keep telling you to do something. *Mom keeps nagging me to tie my shoelaces.*

nail
nails
1 A **nail** is a piece of metal with a point at one end. You use nails to join pieces of wood together.
2 Your **nails** are the hard parts at the ends of your fingers and toes.

naked
Someone who is **naked** is not wearing any clothes.

name
names
A **name** is what you call a person or a thing. *My friend's name is Tim.*

nap
naps
If you take a **nap**, you sleep for a short time.

napkin
napkins
A napkin is a piece of cloth or paper that you use to protect your clothes when you eat. *Katy put the napkins on the table.*

narrate
narrates narrating narrated
If you **narrate** a story, you tell it or read it aloud to someone.

narrow
narrower narrowest
If something is **narrow**, its sides are not far apart. *We rode down the narrow path.*
■ *opposite* **wide**

nasty
nastier nastiest
Someone who is **nasty** is cruel and unkind. *A nasty witch.*

natural
Something that is **natural** has not been made by people or machines. *Wood is a natural material.*

nature
Nature is everything on the earth that has not been made by people. Plants, animals and the weather are all parts of nature.

naughty
naughtier naughtiest
Someone who is **naughty** behaves badly. *Abby was very naughty today. She threw her lunch out of the window.*

near
nearer nearest
If something is **near**, it is only a short distance away. *The park is very near our house.*
■ *opposite* **far**

nearly
Nearly means almost, but not quite. *Jodie is nearly four feet tall. I nearly won the race, but Travis beat me by five seconds.*

neat
neater neatest
1 Something that is **neat** looks tidy and clean. *Carly keeps her room really neat.*
2 **Neat** also means clever. *What a neat trick!*

neck
necks
Your **neck** is the part of your body that joins your head to your shoulders.

necklace
necklaces
A **necklace** is a string of beads or a chain that you wear around your neck.
● *See jewelry on page 59.*

> **Some words that begin** with an "n" sound, such as **knee**, **knife**, **knock** and **know**, are spelled "kn."

need
needs needing needed
If you **need** something, you must have it. *Human beings need food and water to live.*

needle
needles
1 A **needle** is a very thin, pointed piece of metal that you use for sewing. You put thread through a hole in the needle.
2 Knitting **needles** are long sticks made of plastic, wood or metal. People use knitting needles to knit clothes out of yarn.

neighbor
neighbors
A **neighbor** is someone who lives near you.

neighborhood
neighborhoods
A **neighborhood** is an area in a town or a city where people live. *I live in a friendly neighborhood.*

neither
Neither means not one or the other. *Neither of us speak French.*

nephew
nephews
Someone's **nephew** is the son of their sister or their brother.

nervous
1 If you are **nervous** about something, you are worried or excited about it. *Bud is nervous about his first trip in a plane.*
2 A **nervous** person or animal is easily frightened. *Don't scare the kittens. They're very nervous.*

nest
nests
A **nest** is a home made by birds and some animals. Birds keep their eggs and their babies in a nest.

net
nets
1 A **net** is a bag made of knotted thread or rope. Nets are used to catch fish. *Tyler caught some fish in his net and then put them back in the water.*
2 When you play tennis, you hit the ball over a **net**. Tennis nets are made of knotted rope.

never
Never means not at any time. *You must never talk to strangers.*
■ *opposite* **always**

new
newer newest
1 If something is **new**, it has just been made. *A new bike.*
■ *opposite* **old**
2 **New** can also mean different. *There's a new family next door.*

news
1 **News** is information about things that are happening in the world. *Dad always listens to the news on the radio.*
2 **News** is also information about things that have happened to you. *I've had some good news. I've won the art contest.*

newspaper
newspapers
A **newspaper** is made of several sheets of paper with stories and pictures about the news. Most newspapers come out every day.

newt

newts
A **newt** is a small creature with short legs and a long tail. Newts live on land and lay their eggs in water.

next
1 **Next** means the one after this. *We're all going on vacation next week.*
2 **Next** also means nearest. *Jason sits next to me at school.*

nice
nicer nicest
If you think that something is **nice**, you like it. *A nice meal. A nice day.*

> **Some other words for** nice are **beautiful, pleasant, good, lovely** and **enjoyable**.

nickname
nicknames
A **nickname** is a name that you give to a friend. *Jim's nickname is Carrots because he has red hair.*

niece
nieces
Someone's **niece** is the daughter of their sister or their brother.

night
Night is the time when it is dark outside. People sleep at night.

nightgown
nightgowns
A **nightgown** is a loose dress that girls and women wear in bed.

nightmare
nightmares
A **nightmare** is a horrible, frightening dream.

nobody
Nobody means no person. *There was nobody in the house.*

nod
nods nodding nodded
When you **nod**, you move your head up and down. People often nod to show that they agree.

noise
noises
A **noise** is a sound. *We heard a noise coming from the cellar.*

noisy
noisier noisiest
If something is **noisy**, it is very loud. *I wish that Dale's drums were not quite so noisy.*

none
None means not one or not any. *Aaron went to buy some doughnuts, but there were none left.*

nonsense
Something that is **nonsense** is silly and does not mean anything. *Katy is talking nonsense again.*

noon
Noon is 12 o'clock in the middle of the day.

no one
No one means no person. *There was no one in when I got home.*

normal
Something that is **normal** is ordinary and usual. *I got up at the normal time.*

north
North is a direction. If you look at the sun when it rises, north is on your left.

nose
noses
Your **nose** is the part of your face that you use to smell and breathe.

note
notes
1 A **note** is a sound that you make when you sing or play a musical instrument. A piece of music is made up of many different notes.
2 A **note** is also a short message that you write down.
3 A **note** is another name for a bill. *A $5.00 note.*

nothing
Nothing means not a thing. *There was nothing left in Pepper's bowl.*

notice
notices noticing noticed
If you **notice** something, you see it and pay attention to it. *Becky noticed that Eric looked pale.*

now
Now means at this time. *It's raining now, so let's go out later.*

number
numbers
A **number** is a word or a sign that shows you how many there are. Four and thirty-three are numbers. 9 and 27 are also numbers.

nurse
nurses
A **nurse** is someone who looks after people who are sick or hurt. Nurses often work in hospitals.

nursery
nurseries
1 A **nursery** is a room where a baby can sleep and play.
2 A **nursery** is also a place where you can buy plants.

nut
nuts
A **nut** has a hard shell and usually grows on a tree. Many nuts can be eaten.

oar
oars

An **oar** is a long pole with a wide end. You use oars to row a boat.

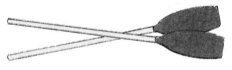

obey
obeys obeying obeyed

When you **obey** someone, you do what they tell you to do. *Garth is teaching his puppy to obey him.*

■ *opposite* **disobey**

object
objects

An **object** is a thing that you can touch and see. Objects are not alive. Computers, toys, books and furniture are all objects.

obvious
If something is **obvious**, it is easy to see or easy to understand.

ocean
oceans

An **ocean** is a very large area of salty water.

o'clock
You use the word **o'clock** when you say what time it is. O'clock is short for of the clock. *It is now seven o'clock.*

octopus
octopuses

An **octopus** is a sea creature with a soft body and eight long arms.

odd
odder oddest

1 An **odd** number cannot be divided exactly by two. 1, 3, 5 and 7 are odd numbers.

■ *opposite* **even**

2 If something is **odd**, it is strange or unusual. *An odd hat.*

3 **Odd** things are not part of a pair or a set. *Odd socks.*

off
1 When you turn **off** a machine, you make it stop working.

■ *opposite* **on**

2 **Off** also means away from something. *Take the plates off the table.*

■ *opposite* **on**

offer
offers offering offered

1 If you **offer** to do something, you say that you will do it. *Hunter offered to make the tea.*

2 If you **offer** someone something, you ask them if they would like it. *Luisa offered a sandwich to her aunt.*

office
offices

An **office** is a room or a building where people work at desks.

often
If you do something **often**, you do it a lot. *We often go skating.*

oil
oils

Oil is a thick liquid. Some oil comes from the ground and is used to work machines and to make heat. Some oil comes from plants and is used for cooking.

old
older oldest

1 Someone who is **old** has lived for a long time. *An old man.*

■ *opposite* **young**

2 Something that is **old** has been used for a long time. *Old clothes.*

■ *opposite* **new**

on
1 When you turn **on** a machine, you make it start working.

■ *opposite* **off**

2 **On** also means touching the surface of something. *Put the plates on the table.*

■ *opposite* **off**

3 **On** also means about. *Sharon bought a book on cats.*

4 You use **on** to say when something happened. *We went out for lunch on Friday.*

once

1 If something happens **once**, it happens one time. *I've only been to New York once.*
2 **Once** also means after. *Once we've had lunch, we can go out.*

onion

onions

An **onion** is a round vegetable with a strong taste and smell. Onions grow under the ground.

only

Only means just one and not any others. *I only have $1.00 left.*

open

opens opening opened
1 If you **open** a door, you move it so that you can go through it.
■ *opposite* **close**
2 If you **open** a box, you take its lid off, so that you can put things in or take things out of it.
■ *opposite* **close**

open

If something is **open**, people can go through it or into it. *The door is open. The store is open all day.*

operation

operations
When someone has an **operation**, part of their body is repaired, replaced or removed.

opposite

opposites
The **opposite** of something is the thing that is most different from it. *The opposite of dark is light.*

opposite

If two people are **opposite** one another, they face each other. *My friend sat opposite me, on the other side of the table.*

orange

oranges
1 **Orange** is the color that you make when you mix red and yellow. Carrots are orange.
2 An **orange** is a round, juicy fruit with a thick, orange skin.

orchard

orchards
An **orchard** is a piece of land where fruit trees are grown.

orchestra

orchestras
An **orchestra** is a large group of people who play different musical instruments together. *The orchestra gave a concert.*

order

Order is the way that things are arranged. *Liza arranged her dolls in order of size, from the smallest to the biggest.*

order

orders ordering ordered
1 If someone **orders** you to do something, they tell you to do it.
2 If you **order** food in a restaurant, you say that you want it.

ordinary

If something is **ordinary**, it is usual and not special. *It was just an ordinary day.*

organ

organs
1 An **organ** is a musical instrument with keys like a piano and lots of pipes of different sizes. When you press the keys, air is pushed through the pipes to make notes.
2 An **organ** is also a part of your body that does a particular job. Your heart and lungs are organs.

organize

organizes organizing organized
When you **organize** something, you plan it so that it happens in the way that you want it to. *We are organizing a party.*

ornament

ornaments
An **ornament** is a small object that is used to decorate something. *Jo hung the ornaments on the Christmas tree.*

ostrich
ostriches
An **ostrich** is a large bird with a long neck and long legs. Ostriches can run very fast, but they cannot fly.

other
1 **Other** means something different. *Do you have any other games?*
2 **Other** also means one of two things. *I can't find my other shoe.*

otter
otters
An **otter** is an animal with brown fur and a long tail. Otters live near water and they catch fish to eat.

ought
If you **ought** to do something, you should do it. *You ought to brush your teeth.*

out
Out means not inside. *We went out for some fresh air. We took the books out of the box.*
■ opposite in

outdoors
If you are **outdoors**, you are not in a building. *In the summer, we play outdoors.*
■ opposite indoors

outing
outings
If you go on an **outing**, you visit somewhere, usually for a day. *We enjoyed our outing to the lake.*

outline
outlines
An **outline** is a line around the edge of something. *Rosa drew an outline of the leaf.*

outside
1 If something is **outside** a thing, it is not in it. *I left my shoes outside my bedroom.*
2 **Outside** also means outdoors. *We went outside as soon as it stopped raining.*

oval
ovals
An **oval** is a shape like an egg.
● See **shapes** on page 106.

oven
ovens
An **oven** is the part of a stove that you use for baking or roasting food.

over
1 **Over** means on top of something. *Juanita wore a vest over her blouse.*
■ opposite under
2 **Over** also means above or across something. *A plane flew over the house. Ed jumped over the pond.*
3 If something is **over**, it is finished. *When the party was over, we went home.*
4 **Over** also means down. *Dean fell over. Kate knocked over the vase.*

overboard
If someone falls **overboard**, they fall off a boat, into the water.

overtake
overtakes overtaking overtook overtaken
When one vehicle **overtakes** another, it goes past it. *Dad overtook a truck on the freeway.*

owe
owes owing owed
If you **owe** someone money, you have to pay them what you have borrowed.

owl
owls
An **owl** is a bird with large eyes. Owls hunt at night.

own
owns owning owned
If you **own** something, it belongs to you. *Richard owns two goldfish and three mice.*

ox
oxen
An **ox** is a large animal with horns. Oxen are often used to carry or pull things.

pack
packs packing packed
When you **pack** a bag or a suitcase, you put things in it.

package
packages
A **package** is something wrapped in paper. Packages are usually sent through the mail.

packet
packets
A **packet** is a small container made from thick paper or plastic. *A packet of seeds.*

pad
pads
1 A **pad** has many pages joined together at one side. You can write or draw on a pad.
2 A **pad** is also a thick piece of soft material.

paddle
paddles
A **paddle** is a long pole with a wide end. You use paddles to row a boat or a canoe.

padlock
padlocks
A **padlock** is a kind of lock. You fasten things together with a padlock to keep them safe. *Lock the shed with a padlock.*

page
pages
A **page** is a piece of paper in a book or a pad.

paid
Paid comes from the word **pay**. *You must pay for your theater ticket. We have already paid for ours.*

pail
pails
You use a **pail** to hold or carry things. A pail has a flat bottom, curved sides and a handle.

pain
Pain is what you feel when you are hurt or sick.

painful
If something is **painful**, it hurts a lot. *A painful knee.*

paint
paints
Paint is a liquid that you use to put color on things.

paint
paints painting painted
1 When you **paint**, you use a brush and paints to make a picture.
2 If you **paint** a room, you put paint on its walls.

pair
pairs
A **pair** is the name for two things that go together. *A pair of socks.*

pajamas
Pajamas is the name for the loose pants and top that some people wear in bed.

palace
palaces
A **palace** is a large house where kings, queens or other very important people live.

pale
paler palest
Pale colors have a lot of white in them. *Melanie painted her room pale blue.*

palm
palms
1 Your **palm** is the flat, inside surface of your hand. Your palm has many lines on it.
2 A **palm** is also a tall tree with large leaves at the top of its trunk. Palms grow in hot countries.

pancake
pancakes
A **pancake** is a kind of thin, flat cake. You make pancakes by frying a mixture of milk, eggs and flour.

panda
pandas
A **panda** is a black and white animal that looks like a bear.

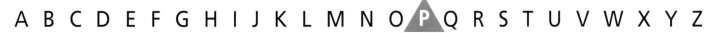

panic
panics panicking panicked
If you **panic**, you have a sudden feeling of fear. *Donna panicked when she couldn't find her mom.*

pant
pants panting panted
When you **pant**, you breathe quickly and loudly because you are out of breath. *Raymond was panting after his run.*

panther
panthers
A **panther** is a leopard, usually a black one.

pantry
pantries
A **pantry** is a small room where you store food.

pants
Pants are clothes that you wear on your legs. Another name for pants is trousers. *Naomi is wearing her favorite purple pants.*

paper
papers
1 **Paper** is the material that is used for writing, making books and wrapping things.
2 **Paper** is short for **newspaper**. *Mom reads the paper every day.*

parachute
parachutes
A **parachute** is a large piece of cloth with strings attached to it. Parachutes are used to drop people or things safely to the ground from a plane.

parade
parades
When people take part in a **parade,** they march together down a street. Music is usually played at parades.

parent
parents
A **parent** is a mother or a father.

park
parks
A **park** is a large piece of land where people can walk or play.

park
parks parking parked
When someone **parks** their car, they leave it on the street or in a parking lot or a garage.

parrot
parrots
A **parrot** is a brightly colored bird with a curved beak. Some parrots can talk.

part
parts
A **part** of a thing belongs to that thing. *Wheels and pedals are parts of a bicycle.*

particular
Particular means this one and not any others. *This particular book is very helpful.*

partner
partners
A **partner** is someone you do something with. *Peter is my dancing partner.*

party
parties
If you have a **party**, you invite your friends to eat and have fun with you. *A birthday party.*

pass
passes passing passed
1 If you **pass** someone or something, you go past them. *We passed you as we drove home.*
2 If you **pass** something to someone, you give it to them. *Pass me your plate please.*
3 If you **pass** a test, you do well in it.

passage
passages
A **passage** is a narrow path, usually between two buildings.

passenger
passengers
A **passenger** is someone who travels in a vehicle and is not the driver.

a b c d e f g h i j k l m n o **p** q r s t u v w x y z

past
The **past** is the period of time that has already happened. *This story is set in the **past** when no one had TVs or telephones.*

past
Past also means by or beside. *The main road goes **past** our house.*

paste
Paste is a soft, sticky mixture that you can spread. *Wallpaper **paste**.*

pastry
Pastry is a food made from flour, butter and water. You roll it flat and use it for making pies.

pat
pats patting patted
If you **pat** something, you touch it gently with your hand. *Scott patted Fido on the back.*

patch
patches
A **patch** is a small piece of cloth that you sew on clothes to cover a hole. *Laura has a patch on her jeans.*

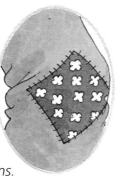

path
paths
A **path** is a narrow road for people to walk along. *This **path** goes through the woods.*

patient
patients
A **patient** is someone who is sick or hurt and is looked after by a doctor or a nurse.

patient
Someone who is **patient** can wait for a long time without getting annoyed.

pattern
patterns
A **pattern** is the way that lines, shapes and colors are arranged. *I like the **pattern** on your dress.*

pause
pauses pausing paused
When you **pause**, you stop what you are doing for a short time.

pavement
pavements
A **pavement** is a hard, smooth surface that covers the ground.

paw
paws
A **paw** is an animal's foot. Dogs and cats have paws.

pay
pays paying paid
If you **pay** someone, you give them money for something.

pea
peas
A **pea** is a small, round, green vegetable. Peas grow in pods.

peaceful
When it is **peaceful**, it is quiet.

peach
peaches
A **peach** is a round, soft fruit with a furry skin. A peach has a pit in the middle of it.

peacock
peacocks
A **peacock** is a large bird with long, colorful tail feathers.

peak
peaks
1 The **peak** of a mountain is the point at its top.
2 The **peak** of a cap is the part at the front that sticks out.

peak

peanut
peanuts
A **peanut** is a small, oval nut. Peanuts have shells and grow under the ground.

pear
pears
A **pear** is a juicy fruit. Pears are rounded at the bottom and get narrower toward the top.

pebble
pebbles
A **pebble** is a smooth, round stone. You find pebbles on beaches.

peculiar
If something is **peculiar**, it is unusual or strange. *Aunt Dottie has a peculiar habit of talking to flowers.*

pedal
pedals
A **pedal** is a part of a bicycle. You press the pedals with your feet to make the bicycle move.

peel
The **peel** on a fruit or a vegetable is its skin. *Orange peel.*

peep
peeps peeping peeped
If you **peep** at something, you have a quick look at it. *Shelley peeped at the sleeping baby.*

peg
pegs
A **peg** is a piece of wood that you hang things from. *Greer hung his hat on a peg.*

pelican
pelicans
A **pelican** is a large bird that eats fish. Pelicans store food in a bag that hangs down from their beak.

pen
pens
You use a **pen** to write or draw in ink. Pens are made from plastic or metal.

pencil
pencils
A **pencil** is a long, thin piece of wood with a black stick in the middle of it, called a lead. You use a pencil to write or draw.

penguin
penguins
A **penguin** is a black and white bird that lives in very cold places. Penguins cannot fly. They use their wings to swim.

people
People are men, women and children.

pepper
You shake **pepper** over your food to give it flavor. Pepper tastes hot.

peppermint
peppermints
A **peppermint** is a candy with a strong, sweet taste.

perch
perches perching perched
Perch means to sit or stand on the edge of something. *The bird perched on the branch.*

perfect
If something is **perfect**, it is exactly right. *Vicky practiced the tune on her recorder until it was perfect.*

performance
performances
A **performance** is something that you do in front of lots of people, such as singing, acting or playing a musical instrument.

perfume
perfumes
Perfume is a liquid that smells nice. People put perfume on their skin.

perhaps
You say **perhaps** when you mean that something is possible, but not certain. *Perhaps we'll see you this weekend.*

period
periods
1 A **period** is a dot that you use in writing. You put a period at the end of a sentence. You also use a period to show that a word, such as Mr., has been shortened.
2 A **period** is also a length of time. *Roberto left the room for a short period.*

permission
If you have **permission** to do something, you are allowed to do it. *I have permission to leave.*

person

A **person** is a man, a woman or a child. *There's room for one more* **person** *in the car.*

persuade

persuades persuading persuaded

If you **persuade** someone to do something, you make them agree to do it. *Allie* **persuaded** *me to wait for her.*

pet

pets

A **pet** is an animal that lives with you at home. Cats and dogs are pets. *Jo keeps guinea pigs as* **pets**.

petal

petals

A **petal** is the white or colored part of a flower. *Rose petals.*

pharmacy

pharmacies

A **pharmacy** is a place where medicines are sold.

phone

phones

Phone is short for telephone.

photograph

photographs

A **photograph** is a picture that you take with a camera.

piano

pianos

A **piano** is a large musical instrument with a row of black and white keys. You press the keys with your fingers to play different notes.

pick

picks picking picked

1 If you **pick** up something, you lift it up. *Kim* **picked** *up the kitten.*
2 When you **pick** something, you choose it. *Pick any cake you want.*
3 If you **pick** fruit or flowers, you take them from a plant or a tree.

picnic

picnics

A **picnic** is a meal that you take with you to eat outdoors.

picture

pictures

A **picture** is a painting, a drawing or a photograph.

pie

pies

A **pie** is a pastry case filled with meat, vegetables or fruit. Pies are baked in an oven.

piece

pieces

A **piece** of something is a part of it. *A* **piece** *of the jigsaw is missing.*

pier

piers

A **pier** is a platform that is built out over water or beside water. Ships and boats tie up at piers.

pig

pigs

A **pig** is an animal with a fat body, short legs and a curly tail.

pigeon

pigeons

A **pigeon** is a gray bird with a fat body and a small head.
▲ *say pij-in*

pile

piles

A **pile** is a lot of things that have been put on top of each other. *A* **pile** *of clothes.*

A B C D E F G H I J K L M N O **P** Q R S T U V W X Y Z

pill
pills

A **pill** is a small, dry piece of medicine. People swallow pills when they are sick to make them well again.

pillow
pillows

A **pillow** is a soft pad that you rest your head on, when you are lying in bed.

pilot
pilots

A **pilot** is someone who flies a plane. *The **pilot** flew his plane over the woods and fields.*

pin
pins

1 A **pin** is a small, thin piece of metal with a point at one end. You use pins to hold pieces of cloth together.
2 A **pin** is also a piece of jewelry or a small picture that you attach to your clothes. *Jenny wore a butterfly **pin** on her jacket.*

pineapple
pineapples

A **pineapple** is a large, oval fruit with a tough skin and pointed leaves at the top. Pineapples are yellow inside.

pink
Pink is the color that you make when you mix red and white. Strawberry ice cream is pink.

pipe
pipes

A **pipe** is a long tube that carries gas or liquids.

pirate
pirates

A **pirate** is someone who attacks ships at sea and steals things from them.

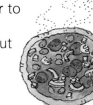

pit
pits

1 A **pit** is a hole in the ground.
2 A **pit** is also the hard seed in the middle of some fruits.

pitch
pitches pitching pitched

When you **pitch**, you throw a ball for someone to hit.

pitcher
pitchers

You use a **pitcher** to hold liquids. You also pour liquid out of a pitcher.

pizza
pizzas

A **pizza** is a flat piece of special bread with tomato sauce, cheese and other foods spread over it. Pizzas are baked in ovens.

place
places

A **place** is somewhere. Places can be very big, like a country, or very small. *Africa is a very hot **place**. Can you find a **place** to put your mug?*

place
places placing placed

If you **place** a thing somewhere, you put it there. ***Place** the vase in the middle of the table.*

plain
plainer plainest

1 Something that is **plain** is ordinary and not decorated. *Gary prefers **plain** food. I have **plain** drapes in my room.*
2 If something is **plain**, it is clear and easy to understand. *Ben made it **plain** that he did not like peas.*

plan
plans

A **plan** is a map of a building or a place. *Katy drew a **plan** of her bedroom.*

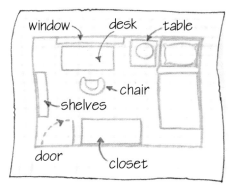

plan
plans planning planned

If you **plan** something, you decide how you will do it. *We **planned** the treasure hunt carefully.*

plane
planes

Plane is short for **airplane**.

planet
planets

A **planet** is a huge, round object that moves around the sun. Earth is a planet.

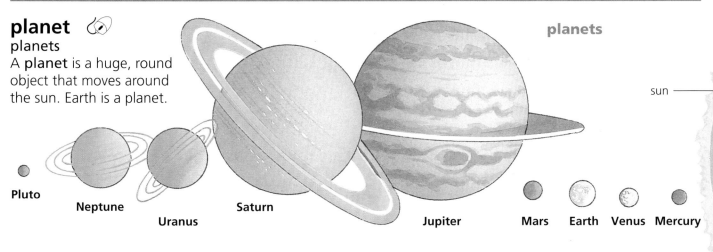

planets

sun

Pluto

Neptune

Uranus

Saturn

Jupiter

Mars Earth Venus Mercury

plank
planks

A **plank** is a long, flat piece of wood.

plant
plants

A **plant** is a living thing that grows in soil or in water. Trees, flowers and seaweed are plants.

plaque
plaques

1 **Plaque** is the white colored coating that sticks to your teeth if you do not brush them. Plaque can make holes in your teeth.

2 A **plaque** is a special plate with writing on it. *The winners will be given a plaque with their names on it.*

plastic
Plastic is a light material that does not break easily. Plastic is used to make bottles and buckets.

plate
plates

A **plate** is a flat dish that you put food on.

platform
platforms

1 A **platform** is a raised area in a room.

2 A **platform** is also the place where you stand to wait for a train.

play
plays

A **play** is a story that you act.

play
plays playing played

1 When you **play**, you do something for fun. *The boys are playing in the park.*

2 If you **play** a sport, you take part in it. *Mickey is playing football.*

3 If you **play** a musical instrument, you use it to make music. *Cassie is playing her recorder.*

playground
playgrounds

A **playground** is a place where you can play outdoors. Playgrounds often have swings and other play equipment.

pleasant
If something is **pleasant**, you enjoy it. *We had a pleasant walk.*

please
pleases pleasing pleased

If you **please** someone, you make them happy. *Carlos pleased his mother by cleaning up his room.*

please
You say **please** when you ask for something in a polite way. *Please may I have an apple?*

plenty
If there is **plenty** of something, there is a lot of it. *We have plenty of food for our picnic.*

plow
plows

A **plow** is a set of sharp blades that are pulled by a tractor. Plows are used to dig up dirt in fields.

A B C D E F G H I J K L M N O **P** Q R S T U V W X Y Z

pluck
plucks plucking plucked
When you **pluck** the strings of a guitar, you pull on them with your fingers to make notes.

plug
plugs
1 A **plug** is a round piece of plastic or rubber. You use a plug to keep water in a sink or a bath.
2 A **plug** is also a small object that connects a machine to the electric power.

plum
plums
A **plum** is a soft fruit with yellow, red or purple skin. A plum has a pit in the middle of it.

plump
plumper plumpest
Someone who is **plump** is a little fat. *A plump baby.*

plus
Plus means add. The sign for plus is +. *Three plus four equals seven.*

pocket
pockets
A **pocket** is a small bag that is sewn on to clothes. You can keep things in your pockets.

pocket money
Pocket money is money that your parents give you to spend.

pod
pods
A **pod** is a part of a plant that contains seeds. Peas and beans grow in pods.

poem
poems
A **poem** is a piece of writing. Poems usually have short lines and often have words that rhyme.

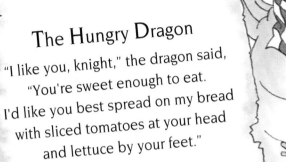

The Hungry Dragon

"I like you, knight," the dragon said,
"You're sweet enough to eat.
I'd like you best spread on my bread
with sliced tomatoes at your head
and lettuce by your feet."

The knight let out a frightened squeal,
"Don't eat me, please!" he said,
"I'd be impossible to peel
and wouldn't make a tasty meal.
Try sausages instead!"

point
points
1 A **point** is the sharp end of something. *A pencil point.*
2 A **point** is also part of a score in a game or a competition. *Our team won by seven points.*

point
points pointing pointed
If you **point** at something, you use your finger to show where it is. *Grace pointed at the squirrels in the bushes.*

poisonous
If you eat something **poisonous**, it can make you very sick or even kill you. Some berries are poisonous.

polar bear
polar bears
A **polar bear** is a large, white bear that lives near the North Pole.

pole
poles
A **pole** is a long piece of wood or metal. *A flag pole.*

police
The **police** protect people and make sure that the law is obeyed.

polish
polishes polishing polished
When you **polish** something, you rub it to make it clean and shiny. *Grant polished his dad's car.*

a b c d e f g h i j k l m n o **p** q r s t u v w x y z

polite
politer politest
A **polite** person has good manners and thinks about other people's feelings.
■ *opposite* rude

pollution
Pollution is damage to the environment. Traffic fumes and litter are types of pollution.

pond
ponds
A **pond** is a small area of water.

pony
ponies
A **pony** is a small, fully grown horse.

pool
pools
1 A **pool** is a small area of water.
2 A **pool** is also a place where people swim. *A public pool.*

poor
poorer poorest
1 People who are **poor** do not have much money.
■ *opposite* rich
2 If something is **poor**, it is not very good. *Poor handwriting.*

pop
pops popping popped
If something **pops**, it explodes with a small bang. *Please don't pop my balloon!*

popcorn
Popcorn is a food that you eat as a snack. When you heat popcorn, the pieces explode with a pop and become large and soft.

popular
Someone who is **popular** is liked by many people. *Jodie is very popular. She has lots of friends.*

porridge
Porridge is oatmeal cooked in milk or water.

port
ports
A **port** is a town with a harbor.

position
positions
1 The **position** of something is the place where it is. *Samantha's house is in a wonderful position, just next to the park.*
2 Someone's **position** is the way that they are standing or sitting.

possession
possessions
A **possession** is something that you own. *Don't leave any of your possessions on the bus.*

possible
If something is **possible**, it can happen or it can be done. *Is it possible to catch a bus into town?*

post
posts
A **post** is a long, thick piece of wood, metal or concrete that is placed firmly into the ground.

post
posts posting posted
If you **post** a message, you put it in a place where people will see it.

postcard
postcards
A **postcard** is a card that you mail without an envelope. Postcards usually have a picture on one side.

Dear Simon,
You wouldn't believe how hot it is here! The ocean is amazingly clear and blue and we've been swimming every day. I've collected lots of shells and seen some really strange creatures in the rock pools.
See you soon,
Kate

POSTCARD

Simon Small
12 Hilltop Road
Bridgeport, CT 06608

poster
posters
A **poster** is a large picture or notice that is stuck on a wall. *Cameron has covered his bedroom wall with posters.*

post office
post offices
A **post office** is a place where you can buy stamps and mail letters and packages.

pot
pots
1 A **pot** is a deep, round container. People use pots for cooking food.
2 A **pot** is also a container for a plant.

potato
potatoes
A **potato** is a rounded vegetable that grows under the ground.

pottery
Pottery is a name for objects, such as bowls and mugs, that are made out of clay.

pound
pounds
A **pound** is a unit of weight. You measure how much a person weighs in pounds. *Alicia weighs 65 pounds.*

pour
pours pouring poured
When you **pour** a liquid, you tip it out of its container.

powder
powders
Powder is made up of lots of very tiny pieces. Flour is a powder.

power
1 If someone has **power**, they control other people or things.
2 **Power** is also the strength or energy that something has. *Dad wants to buy a car with more power.*
3 **Power** is another name for electricity. *Our power was cut off in the storm.*

practice
practices practicing practiced
If you **practice** something, you do it again and again so that you get better at it. *Abby practices playing the trumpet every day.*

precious
1 A **precious** object is worth a lot of money. *Princess Aurora has a chest of precious jewels.*

2 Something that is **precious** is very important or special to you.
▲ *say* **presh**-*us*

prefer
prefers preferring preferred
If you **prefer** something, you like it better than another thing. *I prefer apples to oranges.*

prepare
prepares preparing prepared
If you **prepare**, you get ready. *Mia is preparing for her vacation. Todd is preparing lunch.*

present
presents
1 A **present** is something special that you give to someone.
2 The **present** is the time now. *The story begins in the present.*

president
presidents
A **president** is the leader of a country.

press
presses pressing pressed
If you **press** something, you push it. *Press this button to turn on the TV.*

pretend
pretends pretending pretended
When you **pretend**, you act as if something were true, even though it is not. *Sam pretended that he was asleep. Nicky pretended to be a frog.*

pretty
prettier prettiest
Something that is **pretty** is nice to look at.

prevent
prevents preventing prevented
If you **prevent** something, you stop it from happening. *Jan acted quickly to prevent the accident.*

prey

Prey is a name for the creatures that birds and animals hunt and eat. *The tiger chased after its prey.*

price

prices

The price of something is how much money it costs. *What's the price of this hat?*

prick

pricks pricking pricked

If you prick yourself, something sharp makes a tiny hole in your skin. *Coral has pricked her finger.*

prince

princes

A prince is the son of a king or a queen.

princess

princesses

A princess is the daughter of a king or a queen. The wife of a prince is also called a princess.

print

prints printing printed

1 When someone prints something, they use a machine to put words onto paper. *Mrs. Ross printed my story for me.*
2 When you print, you write with letters that are not joined.

prison

prisons

A prison is a place where people are kept as a punishment, because they have not obeyed the law.

private

If something is private, it belongs to one person only. *A private letter.*

prize

prizes

You win a prize as a reward for doing something well. *Carl won a cup as his prize for coming in first in the race.*

probably

If something will probably happen, it is almost certain to happen. *It will probably rain again tomorrow.*

problem

problems

A problem is something difficult that you need to find an answer to. *We have a problem with our kitten. She keeps running away.*

produce

produces producing produced

1 When you produce something, you make it. *This factory produces tennis balls.*
2 If you produce something, you get it out so that people can see it. *Ginny produced a mouse from her pocket.*

program

programs

1 A program is something that you watch on TV or hear on the radio. *A nature program.*
2 A program is also a set of instructions that tells a computer how to work. *Mom bought a new math program for our computer.*
3 A program is also a small book or a list that tells you about a play or a concert. *The names of all the players are listed in the program.*

progress

When you make progress, you get better or move forward. *Ellen is making good progress at school. The explorers made slow progress through the jungle.*

project

projects

When you do a project, you find out about a subject. *Our class is doing a project on sound.*

promise

promises promising promised

When you promise, you say that you will really do something. *Holly promised to be on time.*

proper

Proper means right or correct. *Is this the proper way to get on a horse?*

protect

protects protecting protected

When you protect someone or something, you keep them safe. *Jo protected her puppy from the rain.*

A B C D E F G H I J K L M N O P Q R S T U V W X Y Z

proud
prouder proudest
If you feel **proud**, you are pleased about what you have done. *Josie is proud of her cake.*

provide
provides providing provided
When you **provide** something, you give people what they need. *The hotel provides lunch.*

public
If something is **public**, everyone can use it. *A public park.*

pudding
puddings
A **pudding** is a creamy food that you eat for dessert or for a snack.

puddle
puddles
A **puddle** is a small pool of water. You see puddles on the ground when it has been raining.

pull
pulls pulling pulled
If you **pull** something, you move it toward you. *Richard pulled his suitcase out of the closet.*

pump
pumps
You use a **pump** to push air or liquid into something. *A bicycle pump.*

pumpkin
pumpkins
A **pumpkin** is a large, round, orange fruit. *Donna cut a face in her pumpkin.*

punch
punches punching punched
If you **punch** something, you hit it with your fist.

punish
punishes punishing punished
If someone **punishes** you, they do something to you because you have been naughty. *Mom punished me for being late by sending me straight to bed.*

puppet
puppets
A **puppet** is a doll that can be made to move. Some puppets are like gloves and you move them with your fingers. Other puppets have strings that you can pull.

puppy
puppies
A **puppy** is a young dog.

purple
Purple is the color that you make when you mix red and blue.

purpose
If you do something on **purpose**, you mean to do it. *Matt kicked his sister on purpose to see if she would cry.*

purr
purrs purring purred
When a cat **purrs**, it makes a low sound in its throat, to show that it is happy.

purse
purses
A **purse** is a bag for money, keys and other small things.

push
pushes pushing pushed
If you **push** something, you move it in front of you or away from you. *Daniel pushed his bike up the hill.*

put
puts putting put
When you **put** a thing somewhere, you move it to that place. *Please put the milk in the refrigerator.*

puzzle
puzzles
A **puzzle** is a game that you have to think about carefully.

How do you get from cold to warm?

Move from cold to warm in three words, by answering the clues and filling in the boxes. For each answer, change just one letter from the word above.

CLUES

1 A type of string.

2 A group of letters.

3 A creature that lives in the ground.

a b c d e f g h i j k l m n o **p** q r s t u v w x y z

puzzle
puzzles puzzling puzzled
If something **puzzles** you, it makes you confused. *Scott's strange message* **puzzled** *me.*

pyramid
pyramids
A **pyramid** is a solid shape with sides shaped like triangles.

quack
quacks quacking quacked
When a duck **quacks**, it opens its beak and makes a loud sound.

quantity
quantities
A **quantity** is an amount or a number. *A large* **quantity** *of sand.*

quarrel
quarrels quarreling quarreled
When people **quarrel**, they argue and get angry with each other. *The boys* **quarreled** *over who should go first.*

quarry
quarries
A **quarry** is a place where stone is dug out of the ground.

quarter
quarters
If something is cut into **quarters**, it is cut into four pieces of the same size.

quarter

queen
queens
A **queen** is a woman who rules a country. Queens come from royal families and are not chosen by the people.

question
questions
A **question** is what you ask when you want to know something.

"What is your name?"

"Where do you live?"

"How can I help you?"

question mark
question marks
A **question mark** is a sign that you put at the end of a sentence to show that it is a question.

quick
quicker quickest
1 Something that is **quick** moves at a great speed.
2 If something is **quick**, it only lasts for a short time. *Mandy took a* **quick** *look around the house.*

quiet
quieter quietest
Someone who is **quiet** does not make much noise.
■ *opposite* **loud**

quite
1 **Quite** means completely. *I haven't* **quite** *finished my book.*
2 **Quite** also means very. *It's* **quite** *cold outside.*

quiz
quizzes
A **quiz** is a game or a test to find out how much you know. You have to answer questions in a quiz.

A B C D E F G H I J K L M N O **P Q** R S T U V W X Y Z

Rr

rabbit
rabbits
A **rabbit** is a small, furry animal with long ears and a short tail. Rabbits live in holes under the ground.

race
races
A **race** is a contest to find out who can go the fastest. *Dale won the race.*

racket
rackets
A **racket** is a bat with strings stretched across it. You use a racket when you play tennis.

radiator
radiators
A **radiator** is used to heat a room. Radiators are made of metal and are usually filled with hot water.

radio
radios
A **radio** is a machine that receives signals through the air and sends out sounds. You can listen to music, plays and news on a radio.

raft
rafts
A **raft** is a kind of flat boat. Rafts are often made from planks of wood that are joined together.

rag
rags
1 A **rag** is a piece of old cloth. You use rags to clean things.
2 **Rags** are also old, torn clothes. *The poor children wore rags and had no shoes.*

raid
raids
A **raid** is a sudden attack on an enemy. *An air raid.*

rail
rails
1 A **rail** is a bar that you can hold on to. *Keep holding onto the rail as you climb the stairs.*
2 **Rails** are long metal bars that trains run on.
3 If you go somewhere by **rail**, you travel on a train.

railroad
railroads
A **railroad** is a track for trains to travel along.

railroad

rain
rains raining rained
When it **rains**, drops of water fall from the clouds.

rainbow
rainbows
A **rainbow** is a curved band of different colors that you sometimes see in the sky. Rainbows appear when the sun shines while it is raining.

raise
raises raising raised
If you **raise** something, you lift it up. *Laura raised her hand to answer the question.*

rake
rakes
A **rake** is a garden tool with a long handle and metal teeth. You use a rake to collect leaves.

ran
Ran comes from the word **run**. *Kitty runs for the school team. She ran in five races last month.*

a b c d e f g h i j k l m n o p q **r** s t u v w x y z

Some words that begin with an "r" sound, such as **wrap**, are spelled "wr."

rare
rarer rarest
If something is **rare**, you do not see it very often. *A rare butterfly.*

raspberry
raspberries
A **raspberry** is a small, red fruit. Raspberries are soft and juicy and grow on bushes.

rat
rats
A **rat** is a small animal with a long tail and sharp teeth. Rats sometimes spread disease.

rather
1 If you would **rather** do something, you want to do it more than something else. *I'd rather go to the beach than do my homework.*
2 **Rather** also means a little. *Henrietta is rather fat.*

raw
Food that is **raw** has not been cooked. *Raw carrots.*

reach
reaches reaching reached
1 When you **reach** for something, you stretch out your hand to touch it. *Toni jumped up to reach the ball.*
2 When you **reach** a place, you arrive there. *It was very late when we reached the hotel.*

read
reads reading read
When you **read**, you look at words and understand what they mean. *Judy is reading to her brother.*

ready
If you are **ready**, you can do something now. *I'm ready to go when you are.*

real
1 Something that is **real** is true.
2 Something that is **real** is not a copy. *A real diamond.*

really
1 **Really** means that something is true. *Men have really walked on the moon.*
2 **Really** also means very. *Whitney was really annoyed that she had missed the bus.*

reason
reasons
If you give a **reason** for something, you explain why it has happened. *The reason I'm late is that my alarm clock didn't work.*

receive
receives receiving received
If you **receive** something, you get something that is given to you or sent to you. *I received your present in the mail this morning.*

recent
Something that is **recent** happened a short time ago.

Oat squares

Ingredients
2 cups oatmeal
1/2 cup butter
1/4 cup raw cane sugar
1 tablespoon corn syrup
1/2 cup raisins

1 Heat the oven to 350°F/180°C.
2 Grease a shallow baking pan 7 x 11 in.
3 Melt the butter, sugar and syrup in a saucepan.
4 Take the saucepan off the heat and stir in the oats and raisins.
5 Pour the mixture into the baking pan and press it down. Bake for 20 minutes.
6 Cut into squares and allow to cool.

recipe
recipes
A **recipe** is a set of instructions that tell you how to make something to eat or drink.

recite
recites reciting recited
When you **recite** something, such as a poem, you remember it and say it aloud.

> **Some words that begin** with an "r" sound, such as **wreck**, are spelled "wr."

recognize
recognizes recognizing recognized
If you **recognize** someone, you see them and know who they are. *I **recognized** Randall easily.*

record
records recording recorded
If you **record** some music or a TV program, you make a copy of it on a tape.

recorder
recorders
A **recorder** is a musical instrument. You blow into a recorder and cover the holes with your fingers to make different notes.

recover
recovers recovering recovered
When you **recover**, you get better after you have been sick.

rectangle
rectangles
A **rectangle** is a shape with four sides and four corners. It has two long sides of the same length and two short sides of the same length.
● *See* **shapes** *on page 106.*

recycle
recycles recycling recycled
If you **recycle** something, you use it again, or you use it to make something new. *Our class is collecting bottles, cans and paper to recycle.*

GLASS   PAPER   METAL

red
Red is a color. Blood and tomatoes are red.

reduce
reduces reducing reduced
If you **reduce** something, you make it smaller. *The toy store has reduced its prices.*

referee
referees
A **referee** makes sure that the players obey the rules of a game.

reflection
reflections
You see a **reflection** when you look in a mirror or look at something shiny.

refreshments
Refreshments are food and drink.

refrigerator
refrigerators
A **refrigerator** is a large machine that keeps food and drinks cool and fresh. *Put the milk in the refrigerator.*

refuse
refuses refusing refused
If you **refuse** to do something, you say that you will not do it. *Tiffany has **refused** my invitation.*

rehearse
rehearses rehearsing rehearsed
When you **rehearse**, you practice something before a performance. *We have been **rehearsing** for the concert all week.*

reindeer
reindeer
A **reindeer** is a kind of deer with large horns called antlers. Reindeer live in very cold places.

reins
Reins are the leather straps that you use to control a horse.

relative
relatives
A **relative** is a member of your family.

relax
relaxes relaxing relaxed
When you **relax**, you rest and stop worrying. *Ashley relaxes by listening to music.*

remain
remains remaining remained
If you **remain** in a place, you stay there. *Dolores **remained** at home while we went to the park.*

remember
remembers remembering remembered
When you **remember** something, you think of it again. *Ryan has remembered where he left his jacket.*
■ *opposite* **forget**

remind
reminds reminding reminded
If you **remind** someone about something, you help them to remember it. *Blake reminded me to send a birthday card to Emily.*

remove
removes removing removed
When you **remove** something, you take it away. *I didn't recognize Sue until she removed her mask.*

rent
rents
If you pay **rent** for a house, you pay money to its owner so that you can live in it.

repair
repairs repairing repaired
When you **repair** something, you mend it so that it can be used again.

repeat
repeats repeating repeated
If you **repeat** something, you say it again or do it again. *Please repeat your name so that I can write it down.*

replace
replaces replacing replaced
1 If you **replace** something, you put another thing in its place. *Damian replaced the broken vase with a new one.*
2 **Replace** also means to put something back where it came from. *Shazia replaced the book on the shelf.*

reply
replies
A **reply** is an answer that you give to someone. Replies can be spoken or written down.

To Anna
Please co...
At 6 Cher...
On Saturda...

212 City Road
Northpool, CA 90102

February 23rd
Dear Michelle,
   Thank you for inviting me to your birthday party. I'd love to come, and I'm really looking forward to it. I've already found the perfect present for you. I can't wait to see your face when you open it!
   Love,
   Anna

reply
replies replying replied
When you **reply**, you give an answer. *"No thank you," Diego replied.*

reptile
reptiles
A **reptile** is an animal with dry, scaly skin. Reptiles lay eggs. Snakes, lizards and crocodiles are reptiles.

require
requires requiring required
If you **require** something, you need it. *You will require paper, scissors and glue to make this model boat.*

rescue
rescues rescuing rescued
If you **rescue** someone, you help them to escape from danger. *The helicopter crew rescued the man from the ocean.*

responsible

1 If you are **responsible** for something, you have to do it. *Al is responsible for feeding Tibbles.*
2 A **responsible** person is sensible and can be trusted.

rest

The **rest** is what is left. *I ate the rest of the pizza the next day.*

rest

rests resting rested
When you **rest**, you sit down or lie down because you are tired.

restaurant

restaurants
A **restaurant** is a place with tables and chairs, where you buy and eat meals.

Some words that begin with an "r" sound, such as **wrestle**, **wrist** and **write**, are spelled "wr."

---

result

results
A **result** is something that happens because of something else. *I got lost and as a result I was late.*

return

returns returning returned
1 If you **return** to a place, you come back to it.
2 If you **return** something, you give it back. *Nat returned the books that he had borrowed.*

reverse

reverses reversing reversed
When someone **reverses** a car, they drive it backward.

revolting

If something is **revolting**, it makes you feel sick. *A revolting smell.*

reward

rewards
A **reward** is something that you are given because you have done something good.

rhinoceros

rhinoceroses
A **rhinoceros** is a large, heavy animal with thick, wrinkled skin. Rhinoceroses have one or two horns on their noses.

rhyme

rhymes rhyming rhymed
Words that **rhyme** end with the same sound. Fight, kite and might all rhyme.

rhythm

rhythms
A **rhythm** is a repeated pattern of sound. Music and poems have rhythm.

rib

ribs
A **rib** is one of the bones that curves around from your back to your chest. Your ribs protect your heart and your lungs.

ribbon

ribbons
A **ribbon** is a long piece of material that you tie around things. *Kate tied some ribbons around the gift.*

rice

Rice is a food that comes from a type of grass plant. Rice grains can be cooked and eaten.

rich

richer richest
People who are **rich** have a lot of money.
■ *opposite* **poor**

riddle

riddles
A **riddle** is a question with a surprising and clever answer.

ride

rides
1 A **ride** is a journey in a vehicle or on an animal. *It's a long car ride to my uncle's house.*
2 When you have a **ride** at a fair, you go on a machine that spins you around or turns you upside down.

ride

rides riding rode ridden
If you **ride** a bicycle or a horse, you sit on it and move along.

ridiculous

Something that is **ridiculous** is very silly. *Elliot looks **ridiculous** in his mom's hat.*

right

1 Something that is **right** is correct and does not have any mistakes in it.
■ *opposite* **wrong**
2 You have a **right** hand and a left hand. Most people draw with their right hand.
■ *opposite* **left**

right ——

ring

rings

A **ring** is a band that you wear on your finger.
● *See* **jewelry** *on page 59.*

ring

rings ringing rang rung
1 When a bell **rings**, it makes a loud noise.
2 When you **ring** a bell, you make it ring. *Ring the doorbell.*

rink

rinks

A **rink** is a place where you can ice skate or roller skate.

rinse

rinses rinsing rinsed
When you **rinse** something, you clean it in water.

rip

rips ripping ripped
If you **rip** something, you tear it. *Sheldon **ripped** his pants on the fence.*

ripe

riper ripest
If food is **ripe**, it is ready to be eaten. *A **ripe** banana.*

rise

rises rising rose risen
When something **rises**, it moves up. *The balloon **rose** into the air.*

risk

risks
If you take a **risk**, you do something that you know could be dangerous or harmful. *Tyrone took a **risk** when he jumped backward into the pool.*

river

rivers
A **river** is a large amount of water running across land. Rivers have banks on either side. They run into lakes or oceans.

road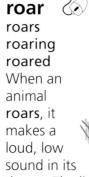

roads
A **road** is a hard strip of ground that goes from one place to another. Vehicles travel on roads.

roar

roars roaring roared
When an animal **roars**, it makes a loud, low sound in its throat. *The lion **roared**.*

roast

roasts roasting roasted
When you **roast** food, you cook it in a hot oven. *Grandma has **roasted** a chicken for dinner.*

rob

robs robbing robbed
People who **rob** take things that do not belong to them. *Three men **robbed** the bank yesterday.*

robin

robins
A **robin** is a bird with a red chest.

robot

robots
A **robot** is a machine that can do some jobs that people do. Some robots look a bit like people.

rock

rocks
1 **Rock** is the very hard part of the earth. Mountains are made of rock.
2 A **rock** is a large stone.

rock

rocks rocking rocked
When you **rock**, you move gently backward and forward or from side to side.

rocket
rockets
A **rocket** is a spacecraft that travels very fast. Rockets take astronauts into space.

rode
Rode comes from the word **ride**. *Candy rides her pony every day. She rode for hours yesterday.*

roll
rolls
1 A **roll** is a small, round piece of bread. *Curtis had a roll with his soup.*
2 A **roll** is also a long piece of paper or tape that has been wrapped around itself many times. *A roll of wallpaper.*

roll
rolls rolling rolled
When something **rolls**, it moves by turning over and over. *The ball rolled down the hill.*

roller skate
roller skates
You wear **roller skates** on your feet to make you go fast. Roller skates have small wheels.

roof
roofs
A **roof** is the top of a building.

room
rooms
1 A **room** is an area inside a building. Rooms usually have four walls and a door.
2 If there is **room** for something, there is enough space for it.

> **Some words that begin** with an "r" sound, such as **wrong**, are spelled "wr."

rooster
roosters
A **rooster** is a male chicken. Roosters make a loud noise when the sun comes up in the morning.

root
roots
A **root** is the part of a plant that grows under the ground. Water travels up the root to the rest of the plant.

rope
ropes
A **rope** is made of lots of threads twisted together. Ropes are often used for pulling things.

rose
roses
A **rose** is a flower with thorns on its stem. Roses often smell nice.

rose
Rose comes from the word **rise**. *We watched the balloon rise into the air. It rose high above the trees.*

rosy
rosier rosiest
If people have **rosy** cheeks, their cheeks look pink. *The boys had rosy cheeks when they came in from playing in the snow.*

rough
rougher roughest
1 If something is **rough**, it is not smooth. *My skin feels rough. The ocean is rough today.*
2 Someone who is **rough** is not gentle. *Don't be so rough, you're hurting me!*
3 A **rough** answer is not exactly correct.

round
rounder roundest
Something that is **round** has a shape like a circle or a ball.

row
rows
1 A **row** is a line of people or things. *A row of chairs.*
▲ *rhymes with so*
2 A **row** is an argument. *We had a row about who should go first.*
▲ *rhymes with how*

row
rows rowing rowed
When you **row**, you use oars to make a boat move through water.
▲ *rhymes with so*

rowboat
rowboats
A **rowboat** is a small boat that you move by rowing.

rub
rubs rubbing rubbed
If you **rub** something, you move your hand or a cloth backward and forward over it.

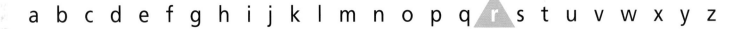

rubber
Rubber is a strong material that can bend and stretch. Rubber is used to make tires, balls and boots.

rude
ruder rudest
Rude people behave badly and are not polite. *It is rude to speak with your mouth full of food.*

rug

rugs
A **rug** is used to cover all or part of a floor. Rugs are often made from wool.

ruin
ruins ruining ruined
If you **ruin** something, you spoil it. *My brother has ruined my picture by scribbling on it.*

rule
rules
A **rule** tells you what you must or must not do. *Games have rules that you must obey.*

rule
rules ruling ruled
Someone who **rules** a country is in charge of it.

ruler
rulers
1 A **ruler** is a flat piece of plastic, wood or metal with straight sides. You use a ruler to draw straight lines or to measure things.
2 A **ruler** is also someone who is in charge of a country.

rumble
rumbles rumbling rumbled
When something **rumbles,** it makes a low sound. *We heard the thunder rumble.*

run
runs running ran run
1 When you **run**, you move quickly, using your legs. *Karen ran after Luke.*

2 When water **runs**, it moves. *The river runs into the ocean.*
3 When a machine **runs**, it works. *This radio runs on batteries.*

rung
Rung comes from the word **ring**. *Can you hear the town bell ring? It has rung every day for 60 years.*

runway
runways
A **runway** is a strip of land where planes take off and land.

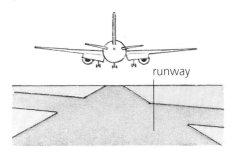

runway

rush
rushes rushing rushed
When you **rush**, you hurry or you do something quickly. *We're late, so we'll have to rush.*

Ss

sack
sacks
A **sack** is a bag made from cloth, plastic or paper. Sacks are used for carrying things.

sad
sadder saddest
If you are **sad**, you feel unhappy. *Russell was sad when his grandparents left.*
■ *opposite* happy

Some other words for **sad** are **unhappy, depressed, upset, miserable** and **glum.**

saddle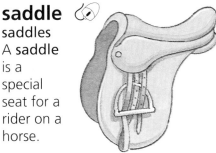
saddles
A **saddle** is a special seat for a rider on a horse.

safe
safer safest
1 If you are **safe**, nothing bad can happen to you. *Inside our house we were safe from the storm.*
2 If something is **safe**, it cannot hurt you. *Dad mended my bike so that it was safe to ride.*

said
Said comes from the word **say**. *Mom asked us to say the alphabet. We said all the letters from A to Z.*

sail
sails

A **sail** is a large piece of cloth that is attached to a mast on a boat. When the wind blows into the sail, it makes the boat move.

sail
sails sailing sailed

If you **sail** somewhere, you travel in a boat or a ship.

salad
salads

A **salad** is a mixture of raw vegetables, such as lettuce and tomato. *Dad has made a delicious salad.*

sale
sales

1 When a store has a **sale**, it sells things for less than their usual price.

2 If something is for **sale**, people can buy it.

salt
People use **salt** to give food flavor. You can add salt when you cook or you can shake it over your food.

same
Things that are the **same** are just like each other. *Freddie's dogs look the same.*

sand
Sand is made of very tiny pieces of rock and shell. Some beaches and deserts are covered with sand.

sandal
sandals

A **sandal** is a light shoe with straps that go over your foot. People wear sandals when it is hot.

sandwich
sandwiches

A **sandwich** is made from two pieces of bread with another food between them. *Sam had ham and lettuce sandwiches for lunch.*

sang
Sang comes from the word **sing**. *Ali often sings in concerts. She sang three songs last night.*

sank
Sank comes from the word **sink**. *The ship hit the rocks and began to sink. It sank to the bottom of the ocean.*

sari
saris

A **sari** is a long piece of light cloth that you wear wrapped around your body. Indian women and girls often wear saris.

sat
Sat comes from the word **sit**. *Kim could not find anywhere to sit. In the end, she sat on the floor.*

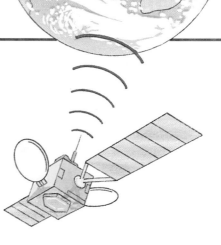

satellite
satellites

1 A **satellite** is a machine that travels around the earth or another planet.

2 A **satellite** is also a natural object that travels around a planet. The moon is a satellite of the earth.

sauce
sauces

A **sauce** is a thick liquid that you eat with other food. *Jason covered his ice cream with chocolate sauce.*

saucepan
saucepans

A **saucepan** is a metal or glass pot that is used for cooking. Saucepans have handles and often have lids.

saucer
saucers

A **saucer** is a small dish that you put under a cup.

sausage
sausages
A **sausage** is made from chopped meat that is put inside a special skin.

save
saves saving saved
1 If you **save** someone, you rescue them from danger. *Lisa jumped into the water to save the child.*
2 If you **save** money, you keep it to use later. *Melanie is saving to buy some paints.*

saw
saws
A **saw** is a tool with a handle and a blade. You use a saw to cut wood.
● *See* **tools** *on page 128.*

saw
Saw comes from the word **see**.
I see my cousin most weeks. Last week I saw her twice .

say
says saying said
If you **say** something, you speak words. *Mark said "Hello" to me.*

scale
scales
1 A **scale** is a set of musical notes that are played or sung in order.
2 A **scale** is also one of the small pieces of skin that cover the body of a fish or a snake.

scales
You use **scales** to find out how much something weighs. *Weigh the plums on the scales.*

scar
scars
A **scar** is a mark on your skin where a wound used to be.

scare
scares scaring scared
If you **scare** someone, you make them feel frightened. *Jessica scared me with her false paw.*

scarf
scarves
A **scarf** is a piece of cloth that you wear around your neck. People wear scarves to keep warm or to look good.

scatter
scatters scattering scattered
When you **scatter** things, you throw them over a large area. *Tommy scattered seed for the birds to eat.*

school
schools
A **school** is a place where people go to learn.

science
When you study **science**, you find out about the earth, space, people, animals and plants. You do experiments to help you learn about science.

scientist
scientists
A **scientist** is someone who does experiments to find out more about the world.

scissors
You use a pair of **scissors** to cut paper or cloth. Scissors have two handles and two blades.

score
scores
The **score** is the number of points that each side wins in a game.

scramble
scrambles scrambling scrambled
1 If you **scramble** something, you mix it up or put it in the wrong order. *Sal scrambled the message.*
2 **Scramble** also means to climb. *Aaron scrambled over the rocks.*

scrap
scraps
A **scrap** is a small piece of something. *A scrap of paper. A scrap of food.*

scrapbook
scrapbooks
A **scrapbook** is a book with plain pages. You stick pictures and photographs in a scrapbook.

scrape

scrapes scraping scraped

If you **scrape** something, you remove some of its surface by dragging something sharp across it. *Jacob scraped the mud off his shoes. Amanda scraped her knee on a rock.*

scratch

scratches scratching scratched

1 If you **scratch** something, you make small cuts in it. *Eugene scratched his arm when he fell into the bushes.*
2 If you **scratch** yourself, you rub a part of you that itches.

scream

screams screaming screamed

When you **scream**, you make a loud, high sound. People scream when they are very frightened, hurt or excited.

screen

screens

A **screen** is a flat surface used for showing pictures. Computers and televisions have screens.

screw

screws

A **screw** is a small piece of pointed metal with a flat top. You twist screws into things to hold them together.

scribble

scribbles scribbling scribbled

If you **scribble**, you write or draw quickly and carelessly. *Marco scribbled a note to his dad.*

scrub

scrubs scrubbing scrubbed

If you **scrub** something, you rub it hard. *Leigh scrubbed the rug to get rid of the stains.*

sea

seas

A **sea** is a very large area of salty water.

sea creature

sea creatures

A **sea creature** is an animal that lives in a sea or ocean.

sea creatures

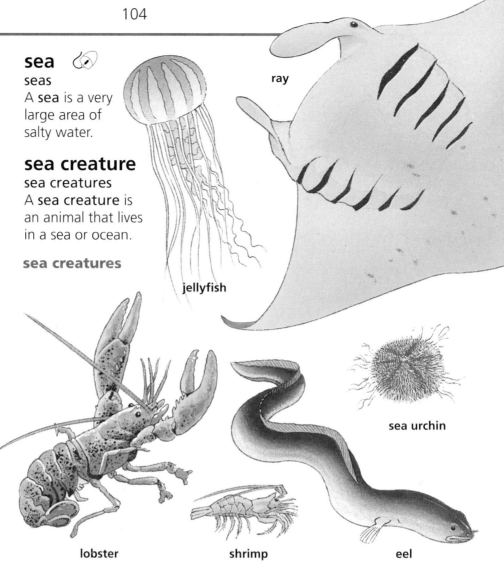

ray

jellyfish

sea urchin

lobster   shrimp   eel

seagull

seagulls

A **seagull** is a large bird that lives near the ocean. Seagulls are usually gray and white.

seal

seals

A **seal** is an animal with smooth fur that lives in the ocean and on land. Seals eat fish and are very good at swimming.

seal

seals sealing sealed

When you **seal** something, you close it tightly.

search

searches searching searched

If you **search** for something, you look for it very carefully.

seasick

People who are **seasick** feel sick when they travel by boat.

season

seasons

A **season** is a part of the year. The four seasons are spring, summer, fall and winter.

a b c d e f g h i j k l m n o p q r s t u v w x y z

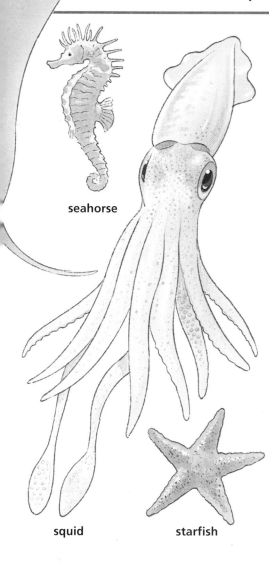

seahorse

squid   starfish

seat
seats
A **seat** is a place where you can sit. *Save a seat for me.*

seat belt
seat belts
A **seat belt** is a strap that you wear around your body in a car, a bus or a plane. Seat belts keep you safe.

seaweed
Seaweed is the name for plants that grow in salty water. There are many types of seaweed.

secret
secrets
A **secret** is something that not many people know. *Cary's birthday present is a secret.*

see
sees seeing saw seen
1 When you **see**, you use your eyes to look at something.
2 When you **see** someone, you meet them. *I saw Suzy in town.*

seed
seeds
A **seed** is a part of a plant. When you put seeds into the ground, new plants grow.

seem
seems seeming seemed
If something **seems** to be a particular way, that is the way it looks or feels. *The journey seemed longer than usual.*

seen
Seen comes from the word **see**. *I want to see Neil. I haven't seen him for weeks.*

selfish
Selfish people think about themselves rather than others.

sell
sells selling sold
Someone who **sells** things gives them to people for money.
■ *opposite* **buy**

send
sends sending sent
If you **send** something, you make it go somewhere. *Josie sent a postcard to her aunt.*

sense
senses
1 Your **senses** help you to find out about the things around you. Your five senses are sight, hearing, touch, taste and smell.
2 If something makes **sense**, you can understand it.

sensible
A **sensible** person thinks carefully and does not do stupid or dangerous things. *Jessie is too sensible to stay out in the storm.*

sent
Sent comes from the word **send**. *I must send a letter to Paul. He sent me two postcards last month.*

sentence
sentences
A **sentence** is a group of words that make sense. When you write a sentence, you start with a capital letter and end with a period.

separate
If two things are **separate**, they are not joined together. *Kelly divided the flowers into two separate bunches.*

series
A **series** is a group of things that are alike and follow each other. *A series of TV programs.*

serious
1 If something is **serious**, it is important and should be thought about carefully. *We must have a serious talk about your work.*
2 A **serious** person does not laugh and joke very much.

serve
serves serving served
If someone **serves** you in a store or a restaurant, they help you to buy what you want.

set
sets
A **set** is a group of things that belong together. *A chess set.*

set
sets setting set
1 If something **sets**, it becomes firm or solid.
2 When you **set** the table, you put knives, forks and spoons on it, ready for a meal.
3 When the sun **sets**, it goes out of sight in the evening.

several
Several means a small number, usually more than three. *Dan has several pairs of jeans.*

sew
sews sewing sewed sewn
When you **sew**, you join pieces of cloth together, using a needle and thread. *Jo is sewing a patch on her jeans.*

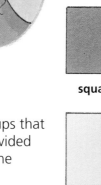

sex
sexes
The **sexes** are the two groups that humans and animals are divided into. One sex is male and the other is female.

shade
Shade is an area that is hidden from sunlight. *Ed sat in the shade.*

shadow
shadows
A **shadow** is a dark shape made by something blocking out the light.

shake
shakes shaking shook shaken
If you **shake** something, you move it up and down or from side to side. *Shake the bottle before you open it.*

shall
Shall means will. *I shall call you tomorrow.*

shallow
shallower shallowest
Something that is **shallow** does not go down very far. *A shallow pool.*
■ opposite **deep**

shampoo
Shampoo is a liquid that you use to wash your hair. You rub it into your hair and then rinse it out.

shape
shapes
The **shape** of something is its outline or the way it looks on the outside.

shapes

square	triangle	circle
		cylinder
rectangle	pentagon	oval
		cube
	hexagon	cone
	diamond	sphere
		pyramid

share
shares sharing shared
1 If you **share** something, you let someone else have some of it. *Juanita shared a doughnut with her sister.*
2 **Share** also means to use something with other people. *I share the computer with the rest of my family.*

shark
sharks
A **shark** is a very large fish with sharp teeth. Sharks are fierce and can attack people.

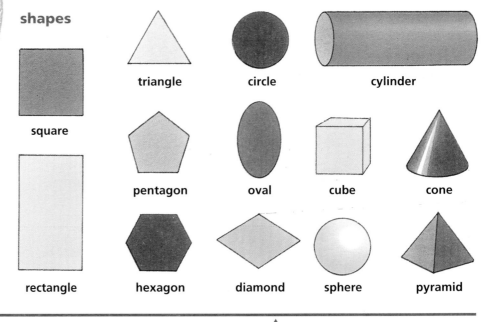

sharp
sharper sharpest
1 Something that is **sharp** has a very thin edge or a point that can cut or prick you. *A sharp knife. Sharp teeth. A sharp pencil.*
2 Something that tastes **sharp** is very strong. *Sharp cheese.*

shave
shaves
shaving
shaved
When people **shave**, they cut hair from their skin. *Grandpa shaves every day.*

shed
sheds
A **shed** is a small, wooden building. People keep tools and bikes in sheds.

sheep
sheep
A **sheep** is a farm animal with a woolly coat. Sheep are kept for their wool and their meat.

sheet
sheets
1 A **sheet** is a large piece of cloth that you use to cover a bed.
2 A **sheet** is also a flat piece of paper, glass or plastic.

shelf
shelves
A **shelf** is a flat piece of wood, plastic or metal that is attached to a wall. You put things on shelves.

shell
shells
A **shell** is a hard cover around something. Eggs, snails and some sea creatures have shells. *Mandy looked for **shells** on the beach.*

she'll
She'll is a short way of saying **she will**. *Mel is finishing her lunch. **She'll** be here soon.*

shelter
shelters
A **shelter** is a place where you can stay dry and safe.

she's
She's is a short way of saying **she is**. *I'm waiting for Courtney to arrive. **She's** coming at 10 o'clock.*

shine
shines shining shone
If something **shines**, it gives off a bright light. *Hold the flashlight so that it **shines** on your face.*

ship
ships
A **ship** is a large boat that carries people and things over the ocean.

shirt
shirts
A **shirt** is a piece of clothing that people wear on the top part of their bodies. Shirts often have a collar and button down the front.

shiver
shivers shivering shivered
When you **shiver**, your body shakes because you are cold or frightened.

shoe
shoes
A **shoe** is something that you wear to cover your foot. Shoes can be made of leather, plastic or cloth.

shone
Shone comes from the word **shine**. *We hoped that the sun would shine all day, but it only **shone** for a few hours.*

shook
Shook comes from the word **shake**. *I asked Craig to shake the orange juice, but he **shook** it too hard and the lid came off.*

shoot
shoots shooting shot
1 **Shoot** means to fire a gun.
2 When you **shoot** in a game such as basketball or soccer, you throw or kick a ball into a net.

shop
shops
A **shop** is a small place where you can buy things.

shore
shores
The **shore** is the land at the edge of an ocean, river or lake. *We pulled the boat onto the **shore**.*

short
shorter shortest
1 Something that is **short** is not very long. *A short time. Short hair.*
2 Someone who is **short** is not very tall.

shorts

Shorts are short pants. People wear shorts when it is hot or when they are playing a sport.

shot
Shot comes from the word **shoot**. *It's Daryl's turn to shoot. Garth has shot three times already in this match.*

should
If you **should** do something, you ought to do it. *You should brush your teeth twice a day.*

shoulder
shoulders
Your **shoulder** is the part of your body between your neck and your arm.

shout
shouts shouting shouted
When you **shout**, you talk very loud. *Kelly shouted to Sarah to pass her the ball.*

shovel
shovels
A **shovel** is a tool that you use to dig. A shovel has a long handle and a flat metal end.

show
shows showing showed shown
1 If you **show** something, you let people see it. *Marcie showed everyone her new watch.*
2 If you **show** someone how to do something, you do it and explain what you are doing. *Anna showed me how to knit.*

shower
showers
1 A **shower** is a short fall of rain.
2 A **shower** is also a piece of equipment that sends out a spray of water. You wash yourself by standing under a shower.

shown
Shown comes from the word **show**. *Dawn wants to show her photographs to the class. She has already shown them to her family.*

shrink
shrinks shrinking shrank shrunk
If something **shrinks**, it gets smaller. *My T-shirt shrank when it was washed.*

shut
shuts shutting shut
1 If you **shut** a door, you move it so that it blocks a space in the wall.
2 If you **shut** a box, you put a lid on it.

shut
If something is **shut**, people or things cannot go into it or through it. *The store is shut on Sundays. The door was shut and locked.*

shy
shyer shyest
If someone is **shy**, they are quiet and find it hard to talk to people they do not know.

sick
If you are **sick**, you are not well.

side
sides
1 A **side** is a surface of an object. *Use both sides of the paper. A cube has six sides.*
2 A **side** is also an edge. *Milly stayed at the side of the pool.*
3 A **side** is also a team. *Which side won the ball game?*

sidewalk
sidewalks
A **sidewalk** is a hard path beside a road. You walk on the sidewalk.

sigh
sighs sighing sighed
When you **sigh**, you breathe out noisily. People usually sigh because they are sad or bored.

sight
sights
A **sight** is something that you see.

sign
signs
1 A **sign** is a shape that means something. *The sign for a dollar is $.*
2 A **sign** is also a set of words or pictures that tell you what to do or where to go. *Picnic places are often marked with a sign.*

sign
signs signing signed
When you **sign** something, you write your name on it.

signal
signals
A **signal** is a message that does not use any words. *The climbers waved their arms as a signal to the rescue helicopter.*

silly
sillier silliest
If you are being **silly**, you are not behaving in a sensible way.

silver
Silver is a shiny, gray metal that is valuable. Some jewelry and coins are made of silver.

similar
If two things are **similar**, they are alike in some ways, but not exactly the same. *Leon and his brother look similar, but Leon has freckles.*

simple
simpler simplest
If something is **simple**, it is very easy to do or to understand.

since
Since means after. *I haven't seen Jodie since Friday.*

sing
sings singing sang sung
When you **sing**, you use your voice to make music. *Jerry loves singing to the radio.*

single
Single means only one. *There was a single rose in the vase.*

sink
sinks
A **sink** is something that you wash things in. Sinks have faucets and a plug. *Grant is washing the plates in the sink.*

sink
sinks sinking sank sunk
If something **sinks**, it moves downward, usually underwater. *Lee's shoe is sinking to the bottom of the stream.*

sip
sips sipping sipped
When you **sip** a drink, you drink a small amount at a time. *Richard sipped his hot chocolate.*

sister
sisters
Your **sister** is a girl who has the same mom and dad as you have.

sit
sits sitting sat
When you **sit**, you rest your bottom on something. *We sat on the steps to wait for Rob.*

size
sizes
The **size** of something is how big or small it is. *What size are your feet?*

skate
skates
Skates are special boots that you wear to move smoothly on ice. Skates have a long piece of metal attached to the bottom of them.

skate
skates skating skated
When you **skate**, you move smoothly on ice, wearing skates.

A B C D E F G H I J K L M N O P Q R **S** T U V W X Y Z

skateboard
skateboards
A **skateboard** is a narrow board with wheels attached to the bottom of it.
You ride a skateboard by standing on it and pushing off with one foot.

skeleton
skeletons
A **skeleton** is all the bones in the body of a person or an animal.

skeleton

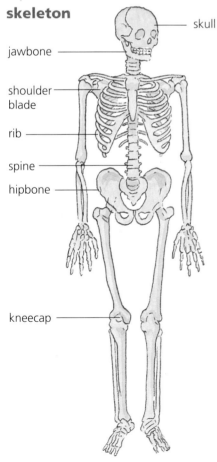

skull
jawbone
shoulder blade
rib
spine
hipbone
kneecap

sketch
sketches sketching sketched
When you **sketch**, you make a quick drawing. *Luisa sketched her brothers while they were skating.*

ski
skis
Skis are long, narrow strips of wood, metal or plastic. You fasten skis to your boots and use them to travel fast over snow.

ski
skis skiing skied
When you **ski**, you travel fast over snow, wearing skis. *Joanna skied down the mountain.*

skid
skids skidding skidded
If you **skid**, you slide on slippery ground. *Noah skidded on the icy sidewalk.*

skill
skills
If you have a **skill**, you are able to do something well. *Sarah's special skill is drawing.*

skin
skins
1 Your body is covered with **skin**. Babies have very smooth skin.
2 The **skin** of a fruit or a vegetable is its outside layer.

skip
skips skipping skipped
1 When you **skip**, you move by hopping first on one foot and then on the other.
2 When you **skip** with a jump rope, you keep swinging the rope over your head and jumping over it.

skirt
skirts
A **skirt** is a piece of clothing worn by women and girls. Skirts hang from the waist.

skull
skulls
Your **skull** is the bony part of your head. Your brain is inside your skull.

sky
The **sky** is the space above the ground. You see clouds and stars in the sky.

slam
slams slamming slammed
When you **slam** a door, you shut it with a bang.

slap
slaps slapping slapped
If you **slap** someone, you hit them with the palm of your hand.

sled
sleds
A **sled** is a small vehicle that you use to ride over snow.

sleep
sleeps sleeping slept
When you **sleep**, you close your eyes and rest your whole body. Most people sleep at night.

sleet
Sleet is icy rain. It looks like wet snow.

sleeve
sleeves
A **sleeve** is the part of a piece of clothing that covers your arm. *This shirt has long sleeves.*

sleigh
sleighs
A **sleigh** is a sled that is pulled by a horse or a reindeer.
▲ *say slay*

slept
Slept comes from the word **sleep**. *Usually, Anna doesn't sleep well, but she slept for hours last night.*

slice
slices
A **slice** is a piece of food that has been cut from a larger piece. *A slice of cake.*

slide
slides
A **slide** is something that you play on in playgrounds. You climb up steps and then slide down.

slide
slides sliding slid
When something **slides**, it moves smoothly over something else. *Jo slid the book across the table.*

slimy
slimier slimiest
Something that is **slimy** is slippery.

slip
slips slipping slipped
If you **slip**, you slide and fall over. *Danny slipped on the wet floor.*

slipper
slippers
A **slipper** is a soft, comfortable shoe that you wear indoors.

slippery
If something is **slippery**, it is difficult to grip or to walk on.

slope
slopes
A **slope** is ground that goes up or down, like the sides of a hill.

slope
slopes sloping sloped
If something **slopes**, it is higher at one end than the other. *The lawn slopes down to the gate.*

slot
slots
A **slot** is a small, narrow space that you put something in. *Put a coin in the slot.*

slow
slower slowest
Something that is **slow** takes a long time to go somewhere or to do something. *A slow train.*
■ *opposite* **fast**

smack
smacks smacking smacked
If you **smack** something, you hit it with the palm of your hand.

small
smaller smallest
Something that is **small** is not as large as other things of the same kind. *A small dog.*
■ *opposite* **big**

> **Some other words for** small are **little, minute, tiny** and **teensy.**

smash
smashes smashing smashed
If something **smashes**, it breaks into lots of pieces because it has been dropped or hit. *The cup smashed when Robert dropped it.*

smell
smells smelling smelled
1 When you **smell** something, you find out about it by using your nose. *Kate smelled the flowers.*
2 If something **smells**, you notice it by using your nose. *That cake smells good.*

smile
smiles smiling smiled
When you **smile**, the corners of your mouth turn up. You smile when you are happy or when you think that something is funny.

smoke
Smoke is a gas that is made when something burns. Smoke looks like a gray cloud.

smooth
smoother smoothest
Something that is **smooth** does not have any bumps or lumps in it. *Smooth skin. A smooth sauce.*

snack
snacks
A **snack** is a small meal that you can eat quickly. *We had a snack when we got home from school.*

snail
snails
A **snail** is a small creature with no legs and a soft body. Snails have shells on their backs.

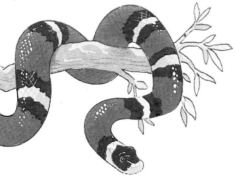

snake
snakes
A **snake** is a long, thin reptile with no legs. Snakes move by sliding their bodies along the ground. Some snakes have poisonous bites.

snap
snaps snapping snapped
When something **snaps**, it breaks with a sudden noise. *The twig snapped when Tim bent it.*

sneaker
sneakers
Sneakers are comfortable, soft shoes. People often wear sneakers for running or for playing sports.

sneeze
sneezes sneezing sneezed
When you **sneeze**, air rushes out of your nose and mouth with a loud noise. You often sneeze when you have a cold.

sniff
sniffs sniffing sniffed
When you **sniff**, you breathe in hard through your nose. Colds can make you sniff.

snore
snores snoring snored
If you **snore**, you breathe noisily through your mouth while you are asleep. *My sister keeps me awake when she snores.*

snow
snows snowing snowed
When it **snows**, small white pieces of ice fall from the sky.

soap
soaps
You mix **soap** with water to wash and clean things.

soccer
Soccer is a game played by two teams. Each team tries to score goals by kicking a ball into a net.

sock
socks
Socks are clothes that you wear on your feet. *A pair of socks.*

sofa
sofas
A **sofa** is a long, comfortable seat for two or more people.

soft
softer softest
1 If something is **soft**, it is not hard or firm. Soft things change shape easily. *A soft pillow.*
■ *opposite* hard

2 **Soft** also means quiet and gentle. *A soft voice.*

soil
Soil is the ground that plants grow in.

sold
Sold comes from the word **sell**. *Jennifer decided to sell her books. She had soon sold them all.*

a b c d e f g h i j k l m n o p q r **s** t u v w x y z

soldier
soldiers
A **soldier** is a member of an army.

solid
1 If something is **solid**, it does not have any air in it. *A solid chocolate egg.*
2 Something that is **solid** does not change shape easily. Solid things are usually hard. Wood and metal are solid.

some
Some means an amount. *We had some soup for lunch.*

somersault
somersaults
When you do a **somersault**, you roll over forward so that your feet go over your head. You can do somersaults on the ground or in the air.

son
sons
A **son** is someone's male child.

song
songs
A **song** is a piece of music with words that you sing.

soon
sooner soonest
If something will happen **soon**, it will happen in a short time. *It will soon be bedtime.*

sore
sorer sorest
If part of your body is **sore**, it hurts. *A sore knee.*

sorry
1 If you feel **sorry** about something, you feel sad about it. *I am sorry that you are not well.*
2 You say you are **sorry** when you are upset that you have done something wrong.

sort
sorts
Things of the same **sort** belong to the same group. *What sort of dog do you like best?*

sound
sounds
A **sound** is something that you hear. *Bees make a buzzing sound.*

soup
soups
Soup is a liquid food that you usually eat hot. Soup is made from meat or vegetables and water.

sour
If something is **sour**, it does not taste sweet. Lemons taste sour.

south
South is a direction. If you look at the sun when it rises, south is on your right.

sow
sows sowing sowed sown
When you **sow** seeds, you put them in soil so that they can grow.

space
spaces
1 A **space** is an empty place or area. *We found a space to park the car.*
2 **Space** is the area outside the earth. The stars and planets are in space.

spacecraft
spacecraft
A **spacecraft** is a vehicle that travels into space. Spacecraft carry astronauts and their equipment.

spaghetti
Spaghetti is a food that looks like long, white strings. People have sauce on spaghetti.

sparkle
sparkles sparkling sparkled
When something **sparkles**, it gives off flashes of bright light. *The diamond sparkled in the sunlight.*

speak
speaks speaking spoke spoken
When you **speak**, you use your voice to make words. *Cameron speaks very clearly.*

special

1 If something is **special**, it is important or better than usual. *A special meal.*
2 Something that is **special** is made to do a particular job. *You need to take special equipment when you go camping.*

speed

The **speed** of something is how fast it moves. *Cheetahs run at an amazing speed.*

spell

spells spelling spelled
When you **spell** a word, you write or say its letters in the right order. *Can you spell my name?*

spend

spends spending spent
1 When you **spend** money, you use it to buy things. *Roberta spent all her money on candy.*
2 If you **spend** time doing something, you use that time to do it. *Josh spent a half-hour practicing the piano.*

spider

spiders
A **spider** is a small creature with eight legs. Spiders make webs to catch insects.

spike

spikes
A **spike** is a sharp point.

spill

spills spilling spilled
If you **spill** a liquid, you let it fall out of its container by accident. *Joel has spilled the milk.*

spin

spins spinning spun
When you **spin** around, you keep turning around quickly. *Melanie spun around as fast as she could.*

spiteful

Someone who is **spiteful** says or does nasty things to upset people.

splash

splashes splashing splashed
When someone **splashes**, they throw water around. *Sharon splashed in the waves.*

split

splits splitting split
If something **splits**, it tears or comes apart. *Judd's shirt has split down the side.*

spoil

spoils spoiling spoilt
If you **spoil** something, you damage it or wreck it.

spoiled

Spoiled children have too many things and are allowed to do what they like too often.

spoke

Spoke comes from the word **speak**. *Warren usually speaks very quietly, but he spoke loudly to the class.*

sponge

sponges
A **sponge** is a soft material with lots of holes in it. Sponges can soak up water and are used for cleaning.

spoon

spoons
You use a **spoon** to eat and cook with. Spoons have a handle and a rounded end for holding food.

sport

sports
A **sport** is a kind of game that you do to have fun and to exercise. Football and tennis are sports.

spot

spots
1 A **spot** is a round mark or shape. *Laura found a spot of dirt on her new dress.*
2 A **spot** is also a special place. *My favorite spot to read is in bed.*

spot
spots spotting spotted
If you **spot** something, you notice it. *Kurt spotted some toadstools in the woods.*

spout
spouts
A **spout** is a kind of tube on a kettle or a teapot. You pour liquid out of a spout.

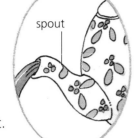

spray
Spray is lots of tiny drops of water or other liquid. *The waves crashed against the rocks and covered us in spray.*

spread
spreads spreading spread
1 If you **spread** out something, you lay it or stretch it over a surface. *Dana spread out the map on the table.*
2 If you **spread** something soft, you put a layer of it on something else. *Spread some butter on your bread.*

3 When you **spread** some news, you tell lots of people about it.

spring
springs
1 **Spring** is one of the four seasons of the year. It comes between winter and summer. In the spring, plants begin to grow and the weather becomes warmer.
2 A **spring** is a piece of wire that is wound into circles. Springs jump back into shape when you press them. Some mattresses have springs inside them.

spun
Spun comes from the word **spin**. *The skater began to spin around. She spun seven times.*

squabble
squabbles
A **squabble** is a silly argument.

square
squares
A **square** is a shape with four sides and four corners. The sides of a square are all the same length.
● See **shapes** on page 106.

squash
squashes
squashing
squashed
If you **squash** something, you press it and make it flatter. *Nat stood on a tomato and squashed it.*

squeal
squeals squealing squealed
When you **squeal**, you make a long, high sound because you are excited or frightened.

squeeze
squeezes squeezing squeezed
When you **squeeze** something, you press its sides together. *Micky squeezed the toothpaste tube.*

squirrel
squirrels
A **squirrel** is a small animal with a big, furry tail. Squirrels live in trees and are very good at jumping.

stable
stables
A **stable** is a building where horses or cows are kept.

stack
stacks stacking stacked
If you **stack** things, you put them one on top of another. *Pablo stacked his books on the table.*

stage
stages
A **stage** is an area in a theater or a hall where plays and concerts are performed.

stain
stains
A **stain** is a mark that is hard to remove.

stairs
Stairs are a set of steps that you use to walk up and down inside a building.

A B C D E F G H I J K L M N O P Q R **S** T U V W X Y Z

stalk
stalks
A **stalk** is the long, central part of a plant. Leaves, flowers and fruit grow from the stalk. Stalk is another word for stem.

stamp
stamps

A **stamp** is a small piece of paper with a picture printed on it. You stick stamps on letters and packages to show that you have paid to mail them.

stamp
stamps stamping stamped
If you **stamp** your foot, you put it down hard on the ground.

stand
stands standing stood
When you **stand**, you are on your feet and upright. *Stand up straight!*

stank
Stank comes from the word **stink**. *My brother's feet stink. After his run, they **stank** even worse than usual.*

star
stars
1 A **star** is a ball of burning gases in space. At night, stars look like tiny points of light in the sky.
2 A **star** is also a shape with points.
3 A **star** is also a famous person, such as an actor or a singer.

stare
stares staring stared
If you **stare** at something, you look at it for a long time with your eyes wide open.

start
starts starting started
When you **start** to do something, you do the first part of it. *Naomi started to do her homework.*

state
states
A **state** is a part of a country. Not all countries have states, but the United States has 50 states.

station
stations

1 A **station** is a place where trains or buses stop.
2 A **station** is also a building used by the police and firefighters.

statue
statues
A **statue** is a large model of a person or an animal. Statues are made from stone, metal or some other hard material.

stay
stays staying stayed
1 If you **stay** in a place, you do not leave it. *We stayed at home all day.*
2 If you **stay** with someone, you live with them for a short time. *We are staying with my uncle for a week.*

steady
steadier steadiest
If something is **steady**, it does not move around or shake. *You need a steady hand to hold the camera still.*

steal
steals stealing stole stolen
People who **steal** take things that do not belong to them.

steam
Steam is water that has boiled and turned into a cloud of tiny water drops.

steel
Steel is a hard, strong metal that is made from iron.

steep
steeper steepest
Something that is **steep** slopes a lot. *Natalie climbed the steep hill.*

steer
steers steering steered
When you **steer** a bicycle, you move its handlebars to make it change direction.

stem
stems
A **stem** is the long, central part of a plant. Leaves, flowers and fruit grow from the stem. Stem is another word for stalk.

step
steps
1 When you take a **step**, you move your foot forward and then put it down.
2 A **step** is a flat surface that you put your foot on when you climb up or down. *There are three steps outside our front door.*

stick
sticks
A **stick** is a long, thin piece of wood.

stick
sticks sticking stuck
1 If you **stick** two things together, you use glue to join them.

2 If you **stick** a pin or a needle into something, you push it in. *Susannah **stuck** a needle into her finger by accident.*

sticker
stickers
A **sticker** is a sticky piece of paper with pictures or writing on it. *Tiffany has stuck animal **stickers** all over her bedroom door.*

stiff
stiffer stiffest
Something that is **stiff** is hard to bend. ***Stiff** cardboard.*

stile
stiles
A **stile** is a kind of step that you use to climb over a wall or a fence. A stile is made of wood or stone.

still
stiller stillest
1 Someone who is **still** is not moving.
2 If something is **still** happening, it has not stopped. *Tara was **still** asleep when Lisa arrived.*

sting
stings stinging stung
If an insect **stings** you, it pricks your skin and leaves some poison in your body.

stink
stinks stinking stank stunk
If something **stinks**, it smells horrible. *This cheese **stinks**!*

stir
stirs stirring stirred
If you **stir** a liquid or a mixture, you move it around with a spoon or a stick. *Paul **stirred** all the ingredients together in a bowl.*

stitch
stitches
A **stitch** is a loop of thread on a piece of cloth. You use a needle and thread to make stitches.

stole
Stole comes from the word **steal**. *Mom told us never to steal. Dan **stole** a pencil and she was angry.*

stomach
stomachs
Your **stomach** is the part of your body where your food goes after you have eaten it.

stone
stones
1 **Stone** is very hard and is found under the ground. Stone is used for building.
2 A **stone** is a small piece of rock that you find on the ground.

stood
Stood comes from the word **stand**. *We had to stand in line for the theater. We **stood** there for a half-hour.*

stool
stools
A **stool** is a seat without a back.

stop
stops stopping stopped
1 If something **stops**, it no longer happens. *It has **stopped** snowing.*
2 When something **stops**, it no longer moves. *The bus **stopped**.*

store
stores
A **store** is a place where you can buy things. *A clothes **store**.*

store
stores storing stored
When you **store** things, you put them away until you need them.

storm
storms
When there is a **storm**, it rains hard and the wind blows. Sometimes there is also thunder and lightning.

A B C D E F G H I J K L M N O P Q R **S** T U V W X Y Z

story
stories
A **story** tells you about something that has happened. Stories can be true or made up.

Cassy the Clumsy Crocodile

Cassy couldn't believe her luck when she got a job at Everglades, the biggest store in town. She tried very hard to be helpful, but the first day she broke twenty cups and saucers and knocked a toy train off its tracks.

Worst of all, she dropped a salad on Mr. Everglade's head. He was furious, but he gave her one last chance, selling jewelry.

Cassy was left in charge of the jewels, but she wasn't alone. Hiding in the shop were the wicked Greedy Boys. As soon as Cassy's back was turned, they grabbed the largest jewel they could find.

Thinking the thieves were customers, Cassy spun around to help them. Her tail caught on a necklace and beads scattered everywhere. The Greedy Boys tripped, but Cassy rushed to help them up. On her way, she knocked over an enormous vase which fell right on top of the thieves!

Mr. Everglade was very pleased that Cassy had caught the thieves. He gave her a new job, testing all the candy and ice cream. At last, Cassy could be really helpful!

stove
stoves
A **stove** is a large metal box that is used for cooking. People cook food in pans on top of a stove or inside it.

straight
straighter straightest
Something that is **straight** does not bend or curve. *Use a ruler to draw a straight line.*

strange
stranger strangest
Strange things are unusual, or are different from what you expect.

strap
straps
A **strap** is a strip of leather or other material. Straps are used to hold things together.

straw
straws
1 **Straw** is the name for dry stalks of plants, such as corn and wheat.
2 A **straw** is a thin plastic tube that you use to suck a drink into your mouth.

strawberry

strawberries
A **strawberry** is a soft, red fruit with tiny, yellow seeds on its skin.

stray
strays
A **stray** is a cat or a dog that is lost.

stream
streams
A **stream** is a small river.

street
streets
A **street** is a road which usually has buildings on both sides.

strength
The **strength** of something is how strong it is.

stretch
stretches
stretching
stretched
1 If you **stretch** something, you make it longer or bigger. *Sam stretched the rubber band until it snapped.*
2 When you **stretch**, you push your arms up or out as far as they will go. *Miriam stretched up high.*

stretcher
stretchers
A **stretcher** is a narrow bed that is used to carry someone who is hurt or sick.

strict
stricter strictest
A **strict** person makes you behave and do what you are told. *Our teacher is very strict.*

strike
strikes striking struck
1 If you **strike** something, you hit it.
2 When you **strike** a match, you light it.
3 When a clock **strikes**, it makes a sound to tell you what time it is. *The clock strikes every hour.*
4 When people **strike**, they stop working, to show that they are unhappy about how they are treated or how much they are paid.

string
strings
1 **String** is thin rope. People use string to tie things together.
2 Some musical instruments have **strings**. You pluck the strings to make notes.

strip
strips
A **strip** is a narrow piece of something, like paper or material. *Tear the paper into strips.*

stripe
stripes
A **stripe** is a line of color. *Harry's shirt has red and white stripes.*

stroke
strokes
stroking
stroked
When you **stroke** an animal, you move your hand over it gently. *Amy stroked the cat.*

strong
stronger strongest
1 A **strong** person can lift heavy things and has a lot of energy.
2 Something that is **strong** does not break easily. *A strong box.*
3 Food with a **strong** taste has a lot of flavor.

struck
Struck comes from the word **strike**. *Our clock strikes every hour. It has just struck seven.*

struggle
struggles struggling struggled
If you **struggle**, you try hard to do something difficult. *Brett is struggling with his homework.*

A B C D E F G H I J K L M N O P Q R **S** T U V W X Y Z

stuck

Stuck comes from the word **stick**. *Stick your pictures in the album. I've **stuck** mine in already.*

student

students

A **student** is someone who goes to school to learn things.

study

studies studying studied

When you **study** something, you learn about it.

stuff

stuffs stuffing stuffed

If you **stuff** something into a bag, you push it in.

stung

Stung comes from the word **sting**. *Carmen is scared that the bee might sting her. She has been **stung** twice before.*

stupid

stupider stupidest

If you are being **stupid**, you do silly things and are not sensible.

subject

subjects

A **subject** is something that you learn about at school. Science and art are subjects.

submarine

submarines

A **submarine** is a boat that can travel under water.

subtract

subtracts subtracting subtracted

When you **subtract**, you take one number away from another. *Annie **subtracted** seven from twelve.*

12-7=5

successful

Someone who is **successful** has done well at something. *A **successful** writer.*

suck

sucks sucking sucked

When you **suck**, you pull in a liquid through your mouth. *Holly **sucked** her juice through a straw.*

sudden

Something **sudden** happens very quickly and is not expected. *We heard a **sudden** shout.*

sugar

You put **sugar** in food or drink to make it taste sweet. Sugar grains are brown or white.

suggest

suggests suggesting suggested

If you **suggest** something, you give someone an idea that might help them. *Bella **suggested** that we should try the other path.*

suit

suits

A **suit** is a set of clothes that are meant to be worn together. Suits are made up of a jacket and pants or a jacket and a skirt.

suitable

Something that is **suitable** is right for a particular job. *Wear **suitable** clothes for painting.*

suitcase

suitcases

You use a **suitcase** to carry your clothes when you travel.

sum

sums

When you add two numbers together, the answer is called the **sum**. *The **sum** of 8 and 2 is 10.*

summer

Summer is one of the four seasons of the year. It comes between spring and fall. Summer is the warmest season of the year.

sun

The **sun** is the large, very bright object that you see in the sky in the daytime. It gives us heat and light. The earth takes a year to travel around the sun.

sunflower

sunflowers

A **sunflower** is a very tall flower with a large center and yellow petals.

sung

Sung comes from the word **sing**. *I love to sing. I have **sung** in several concerts.*

sunglasses

Sunglasses are dark glasses that you wear to protect your eyes from bright sunlight.

sunk

Sunk comes from the word **sink**. *Some things float and others sink. The stone has **sunk** to the bottom of the bucket.*

sunlight

Sunlight is the light that comes from the sun. Most plants need sunlight to grow.

a b c d e f g h i j k l m n o p q r **s** t u v w x y z

sunny
sunnier sunniest
When it is **sunny**, the sun shines.

sunshine
Sunshine is the light that comes from the sun.

supermarket
supermarkets
A **supermarket** is a large store that sells food and other things that you need at home.

supper
suppers
Supper is a meal or a snack that you eat in the evening.

support
supports supporting supported
1 If you **support** something, you hold it so that it does not fall. *Support the baby's head when you hold her.*
2 When you **support** people, you help them. *We supported Carly when she got into trouble.*

suppose
supposes supposing supposed
1 If you **suppose** something will happen, you expect that it will. *I suppose Jade will be late.*
2 If you are **supposed** to do something, someone expects you to do it. *I'm supposed to make my bed every morning.*

sure
If you are **sure** about something, you know that it is right. *I'm sure I've seen that man before.*

surface
surfaces
A **surface** is the outside or top part of something. *The surface of this table is very scratched.*

surfboard
surfboards
A **surfboard** is a light, narrow board that people use to ride on waves in the ocean.

surprise
surprises
A **surprise** is something that you do not expect.

surround
surrounds surrounding surrounded
If something **surrounds** you, it is all around you. *The juggler was surrounded by a crowd.*

swallow
swallows swallowing swallowed
When you **swallow** food, it goes down your throat into your stomach.

swam
Swam comes from the word **swim**. *Isabella tries to swim as often as she can. She swam every day last week.*

swan
swans
A **swan** is a large, white bird with a long neck. Swans swim on rivers and lakes.

swap
swaps swapping swapped
When you **swap** with someone, you give them something of yours and they give you something of theirs. *Freddie and Frankie swapped comic books.*
▲ rhymes with top

sway
sways swaying swayed
If you **sway**, you move from side to side. *Tammy swayed to the music.*

swear
swears swearing swore sworn
1 If you **swear**, you use rude words.
2 If you **swear** to do something, you promise to do it. *Bart made Rick swear to keep silent.*

sweat
sweats sweating sweated
When you **sweat**, water comes out of tiny holes in your skin. You sweat when you are hot or nervous.

sweater
sweaters
A **sweater** is a knitted piece of clothing that covers the top part of your body. Sweaters are often made from wool.

sweatshirt
sweatshirts
A **sweatshirt** is a piece of clothing that covers the top part of your body. Sweatshirts have long sleeves and usually have no collar.

A B C D E F G H I J K L M N O P Q R **S** T U V W X Y Z

sweep
sweeps sweeping swept
When you **sweep** a floor or a path, you brush it with a broom to clean up dirt and other things.

sweet
sweeter sweetest
1　Food that is **sweet** tastes as though it has sugar in it.
2　If something is **sweet**, it is lovely. *A sweet kitten.*
3　If someone is **sweet**, they are kind. *It was sweet of you to call.*

swept
Swept comes from the word **sweep**. *I have to sweep the kitchen floor every day. Yesterday, I swept it twice.*

swift
swifter swiftest
Something that is **swift** is very fast. *That was a swift move.*

swim
swims swimming swam swum
When you **swim**, you move through water using your arms and legs. *Dorita swims for the school team.*

swing
swings
A **swing** is a seat that hangs from ropes or chains. You sit on a swing and make it move backward and forward.
We have a swing hanging from our apple tree.

swing
swings swinging swung
If something **swings**, it moves backward and forward.

switch
switches
You turn or press a **switch** to make something start or stop. *A light switch.*

swollen
Something that is **swollen** is larger than usual. *Pete has a swollen ankle.*

sword
swords
A **sword** has a handle and a long, sharp blade. In the past, soldiers fought with swords.
A toy sword.

swore
Swore comes from the word **swear**. *Sam made me swear to keep his secret. I swore not to tell anyone.*

swum
Swum comes from the word **swim**. *I love to swim in the ocean. I've swum every day this week.*

swung
Swung comes from the word **swing**. *Chelsea started to swing her bag above her head. She swung it several times.*

syrup
Syrup is a thick, sweet liquid. Maple syrup comes from maple trees. *I love syrup on pancakes.*

Tt

table
tables
A **table** is a piece of furniture with legs and a flat top.

tablet
tablets
A **tablet** is a small, dry piece of medicine. People swallow tablets when they are sick to make them well again.

tadpole
tadpoles
A **tadpole** is a small creature that will grow into a frog or a toad. Tadpoles hatch from eggs and live in water.

tail
tails
A **tail** is the part at the end of an animal's body.

take
takes taking took taken
1　**Take** means to move something or carry something. *Take your plate to the kitchen.*
2　**Take** also means to ride in a vehicle. *I take the bus home.*

taken
Taken comes from the word **take**. *Dad takes me to school. He's always taken me there.*

takeout
takeouts
A **takeout** is a meal that you buy and take somewhere else to eat.

tale
tales
A **tale** is a story. *A fairy* **tale**.

talent
talents
If you have a **talent** for something, you do it very well. *Manuel has a* **talent** *for drawing.*

talk
talks talking talked
When you **talk**, you speak to people. *Lauren loves to* **talk** *to her friends on the telephone.*

tall
taller tallest
Something or someone that is **tall** is high above the ground. *A* **tall** *tower.* *A* **tall** *boy.*

tame
tamer tamest
A **tame** animal is not wild and will not hurt people. Tame animals can be kept as pets. *Don't be afraid of my pet rat. He's very* **tame**.
■ *opposite* **wild**

tangerine
tangerines
A **tangerine** is a small, sweet orange that you can peel easily.

tangle
tangles
A **tangle** is a bunch of knots that has been made by accident. *This yarn is full of* **tangles**.

tank
tanks
1 A **tank** is a large container for liquids. *A water* **tank**.
2 A **tank** is also a large, heavy vehicle with a gun. Tanks are used by soldiers.

tantrum
tantrums
If you have a **tantrum**, you get very angry. *Jay had a* **tantrum** *when he lost the game.*

tap
taps tapping tapped
If you **tap** something, you hit it gently. *Jonathan* **tapped** *on the door.*

tape
tapes
1 A **tape** is a long, thin strip of paper, cloth or plastic.
2 A **tape** is also a long strip of plastic with sound or pictures recorded on it. Tapes have plastic cases. *A video* **tape**.

tape measure
tape measures
A **tape measure** is a long, thin strip, marked with inches or centimeters. You use a tape measure to measure things.

tar
Tar is a thick, black liquid that goes hard when it is cold. Tar is used to make roads.

target
targets
A **target** is something that people aim at when they are shooting. *Robin aimed his arrow at the center of the* **target**.

tart
tarts
A **tart** is a pie with no pastry on top. *Fruit* **tarts**.

taste
tastes tasting tasted
When you **taste** food or drink, you put it in your mouth to find out what it is like. *Lee* **tasted** *the soup to see if he liked it.*

tasty
tastier tastiest
Food that is **tasty** has a delicious flavor. *A* **tasty** *pie.*

taught
Taught comes from the word **teach**. *My dad teaches people to swim. He* **taught** *me when I was small.*

taxi
taxis
A **taxi** is a car that you pay to ride in. *We took a* **taxi** *to the station.*

tea
teas
1 **Tea** is a brown drink that you can drink hot or cold.
2 **Tea** is also a small meal that you eat in the afternoon. When you have tea, you eat sweet foods and drink tea.

teabag
teabags
A **teabag** is a small bag of chopped, dried leaves from the tea plant. People pour boiling water over teabags to make tea.

teach
teaches teaching taught
When people **teach** you something, they help you to understand it, or they show you how to do it. *Monica is **teaching** me how to play the piano.*

teacher
teachers
A **teacher** is someone whose job is to teach other people. Teachers usually work in schools. *We have a new **teacher** at our school.*

team
teams
A **team** is a group of people who work together or play a sport together. *Carlos plays on the school baseball **team**.*

teapot
teapots
A **teapot** is a container that people use to make and pour tea. A teapot has a handle, a lid and a spout.

tear
tears
Tears are drops of water that come from your eyes when you cry. *Tears poured down Bonnie's face.*
▲ *rhymes with deer*

tear
tear tearing tore torn
When you **tear** something, you pull one part of it away from the rest. *Doug **tore** his shirt on a nail.*
▲ *rhymes with bare*

tease
teases teasing teased
If you **tease** someone, you say mean things to them and laugh at them.

teddy bear
teddy bears
A **teddy bear** is a soft, furry toy that looks like a bear. *Freddie always sleeps with his teddy bear.*

teenager
teenagers
A **teenager** is someone who is between 13 and 19 years old.

telephone
telephones
A **telephone** is a machine that you use to speak to someone in another place.

telescope
telescopes
A **telescope** makes things that are far away look closer and larger. People use telescopes to look at the stars.

television
televisions
A **television** is a machine that shows pictures and sends out sounds. Televisions receive signals through the air and turn them into pictures and sounds.

tell
tells telling told
1 If you **tell** someone something, you talk to them about it. *Laura **told** me about her vacation.*
2 When someone **tells** you to do something, they say that you must do it. *Mom **told** me to go to bed.*
3 If you can **tell** something, you know it. *I can **tell** that Sam is sad.*

temper
If you lose your **temper**, you get very angry. *Al lost his temper when his radio wouldn't work.*

temperature
temperatures
The **temperature** of something is how hot or cold it is.

tennis
Tennis is a game played by two or four players with rackets and a ball. The players hit the ball to each other over a net.

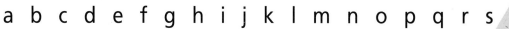

tent
tents
A **tent** is a shelter made of strong material and held up by poles and ropes. You sleep in a tent when you go camping.

term
terms
A **term** is one part of the school year. There are usually two terms in a year.

terrible
If something is **terrible**, it is very bad. *A terrible accident.*

test
tests
You take a **test** to show how much you know about something. *Luis did well in the math test.*

test
tests testing tested
When you **test** something, you try it to see if it works properly. *Elsa tested the new recipe.*

thank
thanks thanking thanked
When you **thank** someone, you tell them you are pleased about something they have done. *I thanked Jim for helping me.*

theater
theaters
A **theater** is a building where you go to see movies or plays.

their
Their means belonging to them. *Do all the players have their soccer shoes with them?*

them
You use the word **them** to mean more than one person or thing. *I wrote six letters last night. Now I need to mail them.*

themselves
Themselves means them and no one else. *The children dressed themselves.*

then
1 **Then** means after. *First drink your milk, then you can go out.*
2 **Then** also means at that time. *I did this painting last year. I wasn't as good then as I am now.*

there
1 **There** means to or at a place. *Have you been there before?*
2 You also use the word **there** to make someone notice something. *There is a cat in that tree.*

there's
There's is a short way of saying there is. *There's lots of food left.*

thermometer
thermometers
You use a **thermometer** to find out how hot or cold something is. *We hung a thermometer in the yard and looked at it every day.*

they
You use the word **they** when you talk about more than one person. *Katy and Kerry are best friends. They go everywhere together.*

they'd
1 **They'd** is a short way of saying they had. *The boys were late because they'd lost their way.*
2 **They'd** is also a short way of saying they would. *The girls promised that they'd return.*

they'll
They'll is a short way of saying they will. *The boys have sent a message that they'll be here soon.*

they're
They're is a short way of saying they are. *The girls are excited because they're going skating.*

they've
They've is a short way of saying they have. *The Robinsons are away. They've gone on a one - week vacation.*

thick
thicker thickest
1 If something is **thick**, it is deep or wide. *A thick book.*
◼ opposite **thin**
2 A **thick** liquid does not pour easily. *This syrup is very thick.*

thief
thieves
Thieves take things that do not belong to them.

thigh
thighs
Your **thigh** is the top part of your leg.

thin
thinner thinnest
1 If something is **thin**, it is narrow. *A **thin** belt.*
■ *opposite* **thick**
2 **Thin** people are not fat and do not weigh very much.
■ *opposite* **fat**

thing
things
A **thing** is an object or an action. *Take your **things** off the table. There are lots of **things** to do.*

think
thinks thinking thought
1 When you **think**, you use your mind. *Try to **think** of the answer.*
2 If you **think** something, you believe it. *Rob **thinks** girls are silly.*

thirsty
thirstier thirstiest
When you are **thirsty**, you want to drink something.

thorn
thorns
A **thorn** is a sharp point on the stalk of a flower or a bush.

— thorn

thought
thoughts
A **thought** is an idea. *Do you have any **thoughts** about what we should do?*

thought
Thought comes from the word **think**. *We tried to think of things to do. We **thought** very hard.*

thread
threads
Thread is very thin cord that is used for sewing and for making cloth.

thread
threads
threading
threaded
When you
thread a
needle, you
pass a thread
through the
hole in its end.

threw
Threw comes from the word **throw**. *Throw the ball to me. Last time you **threw** it to Samantha.*

throat
throats
1 Your **throat** is the front part of your neck.
2 Your **throat** is also the part inside your body that you use to swallow food and to breathe.

throne
thrones
A **throne** is a special chair for a king or a queen.

through
Through means from one side to another. *We wandered **through** the woods.*

throw
throws throwing threw thrown
When you **throw** something, you make it move through the air. *Judy has **thrown** a stick for Fido.*

thumb
thumbs
Your **thumb** is the shortest of your five fingers. You have a thumb on the side of each hand.

thump
thumps thumping thumped
If you **thump** something, you hit it with your fist.

thunder
Thunder is a loud, low sound that you hear when there is a storm.

tick
ticks
1 A **tick** is the sound that a clock or a watch makes.
2 A **tick** is also a small insect that attaches itself to a person or an animal to feed.

ticket
tickets
A **ticket** is a small piece of paper or a card that shows that you have paid for something. *A bus **ticket**.*

tickle
tickles tickling tickled
If you **tickle** someone, you keep touching them with your fingers to make them laugh.

tidy
tidier tidiest
A **tidy** room is neat, with everything in its proper place.

tie
ties
A **tie** is a long strip of material that you wear knotted around your neck.

tie
ties tying tied
Tie means to hold things together with a string, a rope or a ribbon. *Beth **tied** a ribbon around the package. Dan **tied** the boat to the post.*

tiger

tigers
A **tiger** is a large wild cat. Tigers have orange fur with black stripes.

tight
tighter tightest
1 Something that is **tight** is fastened firmly. *A **tight** knot.*
2 Clothes that are **tight** fit closely to your body. ***Tight** pants.*
■ *opposite* **loose**

tights
Tights cover your bottom, legs and feet. They are made out of stretchy material and fit very closely.

time
1 **Time** is how long something takes to happen. Time is measured in minutes, hours and days.
2 The **time** is a particular moment, shown on a clock or a watch. *What **time** is it now?*

timid
Someone who is **timid** is shy and easily frightened.

tin
tins
1 **Tin** is a silver-colored metal.
2 A **tin** is a container made of tin. *A cookie **tin**.*

tiny
tinier tiniest
Something that is **tiny** is very small. *A **tiny** insect.*

tip
tips
The **tip** of something is the end of it. *The **tip** of a match.*

tip
tips tipping tipped
When you **tip** something, you turn it over. *Kenny **tipped** a bucket of water over Katy's head.*

tiptoe
tiptoes tiptoeing tiptoed
When you **tiptoe**, you walk very quietly without putting your heels down. *Stephen **tiptoed** across the hall.*

tire
tires
A **tire** is a circle of strong rubber that fits around a wheel. Tires are usually full of air.

tired
When you are **tired**, you want to rest or sleep.

tissue
tissues
A **tissue** is a piece of soft paper that you use to wipe your nose.

toad

toads
A **toad** is a small creature like a frog. Toads have rough, dry skin and live on land.

toadstool
toadstools
A **toadstool** is a poisonous plant with a rounded top on a stalk.

toast
Toast is bread which is heated until it turns brown.

toaster
toasters
A **toaster** is a machine that heats bread until it turns brown.

toboggan
toboggans
A **toboggan** is a small vehicle that you use to ride over snow.

today
Today is the day that is happening now. *I'm going to a birthday party **today**.*

toe
toes
Your **toes** are the parts at the end of your feet. You have five toes on each foot.

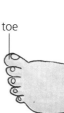
toe

toffee
toffees
A **toffee** is a chewy candy that is made from butter and sugar.

A B C D E F G H I J K L M N O P Q R S T U V W X Y Z

together *to* **to**p
128
For Internet links, go to
www.usborne-quicklinks.com

together

If people do something **together**, they do it with each other. *Sal and Billy played a game **together**.*

toilet

toilets

A **toilet** is a bowl with a seat. When you use the toilet, you get rid of waste food and liquid from your body and they are washed away with water.

told

Told comes from the word **tell**. *Can you tell Joanne to come inside? I've already **told** her twice.*

tomato

tomatoes

 A **tomato** is a soft, juicy fruit with a red skin. You use tomatoes to make salads.

tomorrow

Tomorrow is the day after today. *We're going to the shore **tomorrow**.*

tongue

tongues

Your **tongue** is the long, soft part inside your mouth. You use your tongue to taste, eat and talk.

tongue twister

tongue twisters

A **tongue twister** is a sentence that is very hard to say fast.

She sells seashells on the seashore.

tonight

Tonight is the evening or night of this day. *We're staying in **tonight**.*

tonsils

Your **tonsils** are the two small, soft parts at the back of your mouth.

too

1 **Too** means also. *I'm here, **too**.*
2 **Too** also means more than enough. *The music is **too** loud.*

took

Took comes from the word **take**. *The baby sitter said we could take a cookie. Ian **took** four!*

tool

tools

A **tool** is something that you use to do a job.

tools

tooth

teeth

1 A **tooth** is one of the hard, white things inside your mouth. You use your teeth to bite and chew food.
2 A **tooth** is also one of a row of thin parts on a comb or a zipper.

toothbrush

toothbrushes

A **toothbrush** is a small brush with a long handle. You use a toothbrush to brush your teeth.

toothpaste

Toothpaste is a thick paste that you use when you brush your teeth.

top

tops

1 The **top** is the highest point of something. *Carlos climbed to the **top** of the mountain.*
■ opposite **bottom**
2 The **top** of an object is also a kind of cap that fits over its end. *A pen **top**.*

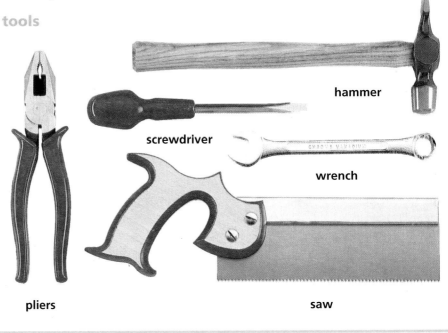

hammer

screwdriver

wrench

pliers

saw

a b c d e f g h i j k l m n o p q r s t u v w x y z

topic
topics

A **topic** is the name for something that you study. Children work on topics at school. *This month, the class **topic** is weather.*

Hurricanes

Hurricanes are very strong winds. They are like huge spinning wheels of clouds, wind and rain. A hurricane can break up buildings and knock down trees.

Main hurricane

Weather diary
Tuesday April 4th
Rain all day
We measured 2 inches of water in our rain collecting bottle.
Wednesday April 5th
Sunny and windy.
Our windmill turned around 40 times in one minute.

tore

Tore comes from the word **tear**. *Scott must try not to tear his pants. He **tore** his last pair when he went exploring.*

tortoise
tortoises

A **tortoise** is an animal with thick, scaly skin and a shell on its back. Tortoises move very slowly.

toss
tosses tossing tossed

If you **toss** something, you throw it into the air. *Megan **tossed** the pancake and caught it in the pan.*

total
totals

The **total** of something is all that you have. *Our class collected a **total** of 150 bottles to recycle.*

touch
touches touching touched

If you **touch** something, you feel it with part of your body.

tough
tougher toughest

1 Something that is **tough** is hard to break or damage. *You'll need **tough** boots for this climb.*
2 Someone who is **tough** is strong and is not afraid of getting hurt.

tow
tows towing towed
When one vehicle **tows** another, it pulls it along. *The truck **towed** our car away.*

toward
Toward means in the direction of something. *Abigail ran **toward** the stream.*

towel
towels
A **towel** is a thick, soft piece of cloth that you use to dry your body.

tower
towers
A **tower** is a tall, narrow building or part of a building.

town
towns
A **town** is a place where many people live and work. Towns have houses, offices, schools and stores.

toy
toys
A **toy** is something that you play with.

trace
traces tracing traced
When you **trace** a picture, you put a thin piece of paper over it and draw around its outline.

track
tracks
1 A **track** is the set of rails that a train runs along.
2 **Tracks** are marks left by the feet of a person or an animal. *We followed the fox's **tracks**.*

tractor
tractors
A **tractor** is a strong vehicle with very large back wheels. Tractors are used on farms to pull machinery or heavy loads.

traffic
Traffic is the name for all the vehicles traveling on the roads at the same time. *There's a lot of **traffic** in the center of town.*

traffic lights
Traffic lights are a set of lights that show traffic when to stop and go. Traffic lights are red, yellow and green.

train
trains
A **train** carries people and things along a railroad track.

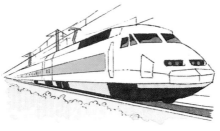

train
trains training trained
If you **train** an animal or a person, you teach them to do something.

trample
tramples trampling trampled
If you **trample** on something, you step on it and damage it. *Don't **trample** all over the roses.*

trampoline
trampolines
A **trampoline** is a large piece of strong material attached to a frame with springs. You jump up and down on a trampoline.

transparent
If something is **transparent**, it is clear and you can see through it. Glass and water are transparent.

trap
traps
A **trap is** something that you use to catch an animal or a person.

trap
traps trapping trapped
If you **trap** something, you catch it. *The spider has **trapped** a fly in its web.*

trash
Trash is the name for things that you throw away because you don't want them any more. Another name for trash is garbage.

travel
travels traveling traveled
When you **travel**, you go from one place to another. *We **travel** to school by car.*

tray
trays
A **tray** is a flat piece of wood, metal or plastic that you use to carry food and drink.

treasure

Treasure is a name for valuable things, such as gold and jewels. *The pirates buried a chest full of treasure.*

treat
treats
A **treat** is a special present or a trip to somewhere nice. *Mom took us to the movies as a treat.*

treat
treats treating treated
1 The way you **treat** people is the way you behave toward them. *Jonah treats his little sister very well.*
2 When doctors **treat** people who are sick, they try to make them better.

tree
trees
A **tree** is a very large plant with leaves, branches and a trunk.

triangle
triangles
1 A **triangle** is a shape with three straight sides.
● *See* **shapes** *on page 106.*
2 A **triangle** is also a musical instrument that is made of metal and shaped like a triangle. You play the triangle by hitting it with a metal stick.
● *See* **musical instruments** *on page 75.*

trick
tricks
1 If you do a **trick**, you do something clever and surprising.
2 If you play a **trick** on someone, you make them believe something that is not true.

tricycle
tricycles
A **tricycle** is like a bicycle, but has two wheels at the back and one at the front.

tried
Tried comes from the word **try**. *Lewis will try to move the box. He has tried twice already.*

trip
trips
When you go on a **trip**, you travel to a place and then come back. *We went on a trip to the zoo.*

trip
trips tripping tripped
If you **trip**, you hit your foot on something and fall or nearly fall. *Natasha tripped over the toys on the floor.*

trolley
trolleys
A **trolley** is a kind of bus that travels on rails in the road.

trophy
trophies
A **trophy** is a prize that you are given for doing something well. *Our team won the swimming trophy.*

trot
trots trotting trotted
If a person or an animal **trots**, they run slowly but smoothly. *The pony trotted around the field.*

trouble
1 **Trouble** is something that is difficult or dangerous. *The farmer had trouble rescuing his sheep.*
2 If you are in **trouble**, you have done something wrong and someone is angry with you.

truck
trucks
A **truck** is a large vehicle that carries things from place to place. *When we moved house, we put our furniture in a truck.*

true
truer truest
1 If something is **true**, it is correct or right.
■ *opposite* **false**
2 If a story is **true**, it really happened.

trumpet
trumpets
A **trumpet** is a musical instrument made of metal. You play a trumpet by blowing into it.
● *See* **musical instruments** *on page 74.*

trunk
trunks
1 A **trunk** is the thick stem of a tree.
2 An elephant's **trunk** is its long nose. Elephants use their trunks to suck up water and to pick up things.

trunk

3 A **trunk** is also a large box that you keep things in.

A B C D E F G H I J K L M N O P Q R S T U V W X Y Z

trust
trusts trusting trusted
If you **trust** someone, you think that they are honest and will keep their promises.

truth
If you tell the **truth**, what you say is true.

try
tries trying tried
1 When you **try** to do something, you do it as well as you can.
2 If you **try** something, you test it to see what it is like.

T-shirt
T-shirts
A **T-shirt** is a piece of clothing that you wear on the top part of your body. T-shirts usually have short sleeves and no collar.

tub
tubs
1 A **tub** is a container that is used to store things. Tubs can be made of plastic, metal or wood.
2 You sit in a **tub** when you take a bath. Tub is short for bathtub.

tube
tubes
1 A **tube** is a long, hollow piece of metal, plastic or rubber.
2 A **tube** is also a container for soft mixtures, such as toothpaste.

tug
tugs tugging tugged
If you **tug** at something, you pull it hard. *The children tugged on the rope.*

tune
tunes
A **tune** is a group of musical notes arranged in a special order. Tunes are usually pleasant to listen to.

tunnel
tunnels
A **tunnel** is a long passage under the ground.

turban
turbans
A **turban** is a long piece of cloth that some men and boys wear wrapped around their heads.

turkey
turkeys
1 A **turkey** is a large bird that is kept on a farm.
2 **Turkey** is also a kind of meat that comes from turkeys.

turn
turns
If it is your **turn** to do something, it is your chance to do it. *It's Bud's turn to use the computer.*

turn
turns turning turned
1 When you **turn**, you move in a different direction. *Turn left at the traffic lights.*
2 If something **turns**, it moves around in a circle. *The wheels turned slowly.*
3 If you **turn** a machine on or off, you make it start or stop.
4 If a thing **turns** into something else, it changes into it. *The ice turned into water.*

turtle
turtles
A **turtle** is an animal with thick, scaly skin and a shell on its back. Turtles can walk on land and swim in water.

TV
TV is short for television. *What is your favorite TV program?*

twice
If something happens **twice**, it happens two times.

twig
twigs
A **twig** is a small, thin branch on a tree or a bush.

twin
twins
Twins are two children who have the same mother and were born on the same day. Twins often look alike.

twinkle
twinkles twinkling twinkled
If something **twinkles**, it shines with flashes of bright light. *The stars twinkled in the night sky.*

twist
twists twisting twisted
When you **twist** something, you turn it around.

tying
Tying comes from the word **tie**. *Kim is learning to tie knots. She has been tying knots for hours.*

type
types
Things of the same **type** belong to the same group. *Daisies are a type of flower.*

type
types typing typed
When you **type**, you write something using a computer.

Uu

ugly
uglier ugliest
Something that is **ugly** is not nice to look at. *An **ugly** building. An **ugly** monster.*

umbrella
umbrellas
You hold an **umbrella** over your head to keep off the rain. An umbrella is made of a piece of cloth or plastic stretched over a frame.

unable
If you are **unable** to do something, you cannot do it. *Travis is **unable** to come tonight.*

uncle
uncles
Your **uncle** is the brother of your mom or your dad. Your aunt's husband is also your uncle.

uncomfortable
If something is **uncomfortable**, it does not feel good. *Uncomfortable shoes. An uncomfortable chair.*

under
If something is **under** another thing, it is lower than it. *Pickle crawled **under** the gate.*
■ *opposite* **over**

underground
If something is **underground**, it is below the surface of the ground. *Wild rabbits live **underground**.*

underline
underlines underlining underlined
If you **underline** something, you draw a line under it. *Underline all the most important words.*

underneath
If one thing is **underneath** another thing, it is in a lower place. *My toys are **underneath** my bed.*

understand
understands understanding understood
If you **understand** something, you know what it means or how it works.

underwear
Underwear is the name for the clothes that you wear under your other clothes.

undress
undresses undressing undressed
When you **undress**, you take off your clothes.

unemployed
Someone who is **unemployed** does not have a paid job.

unexpected
If something is **unexpected**, you did not know it was going to happen.

unfair
unfairer unfairest
If something is **unfair**, it is not right. *Mitchell thinks it is **unfair** that his sister has more pocket money than he has.*

unhappy
unhappier unhappiest
If you are **unhappy**, you are sad or upset.

uniform
uniforms
A **uniform** is a special set of clothes worn by all the members of a group. *A school **uniform**.*

unit
units
A **unit** is a fixed amount of something. Units are used for counting or for measuring things. *A minute is a **unit** of time. A dollar is a **unit** of money.*

universe
The **universe** is everything that is in space. The sun, the moon, the stars and Earth are all parts of the universe.

unkind
unkinder unkindest
An **unkind** person is unpleasant and not helpful.

unlucky
unluckier unluckiest
If you are **unlucky**, bad things happen to you that are not your fault.

unpleasant
If something is **unpleasant**, it is horrible or nasty.

A B C D E F G H I J K L M N O P Q R S T U V W X Y Z

untidy
untidier untidiest
If something is **untidy**, it is messy and not neat.

until
Until means up to the time that something happens. *I'm taking care of Tim's hamster until he comes back from vacation.*

unusual
If something is **unusual**, it is not normal, or is not what you would expect. *Sylvia was wearing an unusual hat. It's unusual for Pedro to be so late.*

up
When something moves **up**, it goes from a lower place to a higher place. *We pushed our bikes up the hill.*
■ **opposite** down

upon
Upon means on. *The cat sat upon the step.*

upright
Upright means standing up straight. *The teacher told the dance class to stand upright.*

upset
If you are **upset**, you are unhappy or angry. *Grace was very upset when her cat died.*

upside down
1 If you turn something **upside down**, you put its top where its bottom should be. *Leon turned the pail upside down to make a seat.*
2 If you hang **upside down**, your head is below your feet.

urgent
If something is **urgent**, you need to do something about it quickly.

use
uses using used
When you **use** something, you do a job with it. *Jeremy used a pair of scissors to cut the string.*

useful
If something is **useful**, it helps you to do something.

usual
Something that is **usual** is normal and you expect it. *I'll be home at the usual time.*

usually
If something **usually** happens, it nearly always happens.

Vv

vacation
vacations
A **vacation** is a time when you do not have to work or go to school. People often spend their vacations away from home. *This year, we're taking our vacation in California.*

valley
valleys
A **valley** is an area of low ground between hills or mountains. Rivers often run through valleys.

valley

valuable
1 Something that is **valuable** is worth a lot of money. *Mom has a valuable ring.*
2 **Valuable** also means very important. *Valuable information.*

van
vans
A **van** is a covered truck. Large vans carry animals and furniture. Small vans carry people and small things.

vanish
vanishes vanishing vanished
If something **vanishes**, it disappears suddenly.

vase
vases
A **vase** is a kind of jar. *Maddy arranged some flowers in a vase.*

VCR
VCRs
A **VCR** is a machine that you use to record and watch video tapes. VCR is short for video cassette recorder.

vegetable
vegetables
A **vegetable** is a plant that you can eat. Potatoes, carrots and peas are all vegetables.

vegetarian
vegetarians
A **vegetarian** is someone who does not eat meat or fish.

vehicle
vehicles
A **vehicle** is a machine that carries people or things from one place to another. Bicycles, cars and trains are all vehicles.

velvet
Velvet is a very soft, thick cloth. People use velvet to make clothes, cushions and drapes.

very
Very means a lot. *I am very excited about going to camp.*

vest
vests
A **vest** is a short jacket with no sleeves. You wear a vest over a shirt or a blouse.

vet
vets
A **vet** takes care of animals. Vet is short for veterinarian.

video
videos
A **video** is a tape with sound and pictures recorded on it. You watch videos on a TV screen.

video game
video games
A **video game** is a game that you play on a TV screen or on a computer. You use special controls to move pictures on the screen.

view
views
1 A **view** is what you can see from a place. *A view of the ocean.*

2 A **view** is also what you think about something. *What's your view of this book?*

village
villages
A **village** is a small group of houses and other buildings in the country.

vinegar
Vinegar is a liquid that you use to give food flavor. Vinegar tastes sour.

violent
If something is **violent**, it is very strong and damages things. *A violent storm.*

violin
violins
A **violin** is a musical instrument with strings. You hold a violin under your chin and move a bow across its strings.
● *See* **musical instruments** *on page 74.*

visit
visits visiting visited
If you **visit** someone, you go to see them. *I visited my grandma yesterday afternoon.*

visitor
visitors
A **visitor** is someone who comes to your house to see you or to stay with you.

vital
If something is **vital**, it is very important. *Vital information.*

vitamin
vitamins
Vitamins are found in food. You need vitamins to stay healthy.

voice
voices
Your **voice** is the sound that you make when you talk or sing. *Ruth has a high voice.*

volcano
volcanoes
A **volcano** is a mountain with a hole in the top. Sometimes hot rock and gas burst out of a volcano.

volume
volumes
1 The **volume** of a sound is how loud it is.
2 The **volume** of an object is how much space it takes up.
3 A **volume** is one of a set of books. *This set of encyclopedias has six volumes.*

volunteer
volunteers
A **volunteer** is someone who offers to do something.

vote
votes voting voted
1 When you **vote**, you show whether you agree or disagree with something.
2 When you **vote** for a person, you show that you support them.

vowel
vowels
A **vowel** is one of the letters a, e, i, o or u.

voyage
voyages
A **voyage** is a long journey.

wade
wades wading waded
When you **wade**, you walk through water.

wagon
wagons
1 A **wagon** was a vehicle used in the past for carrying loads. Wagons had four wheels and were often pulled by horses.

2 A **wagon** is also a toy vehicle. Wagons have four wheels and a long handle that is used to pull them. *Marco has filled his wagon with toys.*

waist
waists
Your **waist** is the narrow, middle part of your body, below your chest. *Sasha tied a ribbon around her waist.*

wait
waits waiting waited
When you **wait**, you stay in a place until something happens. *Simon waited for Sue to arrive at the station.*

waiter
waiters
A **waiter** is a man who serves people with food or drink in a restaurant or a café.

waitress
waitresses
A **waitress** is a woman who serves people with food or drink in a restaurant or a café.

wake
wakes waking woke woken
When you **wake**, you stop sleeping. *Josie woke up early.*

walk
walks walking walked
When you **walk**, you move along by putting one foot in front of the other. *Kay always walks to school.*

> **Some other words for**
> **walk** are **stride**, **stroll**,
> **march** and **hike**.

wall
walls
1 A **wall** is one side of a room or a building.
2 **Walls** are also used to divide areas of land. They are often made of brick or stone.

wallpaper
wallpapers
Wallpaper is paper that people stick to walls. Wallpaper sometimes has patterns on it.

wander
wanders wandering wandered
If you **wander**, you walk around without deciding where to go. *Jonathan **wandered** around the town.*

want
wants wanting wanted
If you **want** something, you need it or you would like it. *I **want** some water to wash the car. Helen **wanted** some chocolate.*

war
wars
In a **war**, armies fight each other.

warm
warmer warmest
Something that is **warm** feels a little hot. *A **warm** day.*

warn
warns warning warned
If you **warn** someone, you tell them about something dangerous or bad that might happen. *Stephan **warned** us that the path was very steep.*

was
Was comes from the word **be**. *I will be at the swimming pool. I **was** there yesterday, too.*

wash
washes washing washed
When you **wash** something, you clean it with soap and water. *Mittie and Dan **washed** their dad's car.*

washing machine
washing machines
A **washing machine** is a machine that washes clothes.

wasn't
Wasn't is a short way of saying **was not**. *Rachel **wasn't** interested in playing the game.*

wasp

wasps
A **wasp** is a flying insect that can sting.

waste
wastes wasting wasted
If you **waste** something, you use too much of it on something that is not important. *Don't **waste** your money on candy.*

watch
watches
A **watch** is a small clock that you wear on your wrist.

watch
watches watching watched
If you **watch** something, you look at it to see what happens. *The children **watched** the parade.*

water
Water is the clear liquid in rivers, oceans and rain. Water also comes out of faucets. People need water to live.

waterfall
waterfalls
A **waterfall** is a place where water from a river falls over rocks.

watering can
watering cans
A **watering can** is a container with a handle and a long spout. You use a watering can to water plants.

watermelon
watermelons
A **watermelon** is a large, round, fruit with a thick green skin. Watermelons are very juicy. They are usually pink inside.

waterproof
If something is **waterproof**, it keeps water out.

wave
waves
A **wave** is the water that rises and falls on the surface of the sea. *The children jumped over the **waves**.*

wave
waves waving waved
When you **wave**, you move your hand from side to side. You wave to say hello or goodbye.

wavy
wavy wavier waviest
Wavy means not straight. *Wavy hair. A **wavy** line.*

wax
Wax is a soft material that melts when it is heated. Wax is used to make candles and crayons.

wax

way
ways
1 The **way** you do something is how you do it. *Is this the right **way** to spell your name?*
2 The **way** you go somewhere is how you get from one place to another. *Which is the **way** home?*

weak
weaker weakest
1 A **weak** person is not strong and does not have much energy.
2 Something that is **weak** breaks easily. *This chair has **weak** legs.*

wealthy
wealthier wealthiest
If someone is **wealthy**, they have a lot of money.

weapon
weapons
Soldiers use **weapons** when they fight. Guns and swords are weapons.

wear
wears wearing wore worn
1 When you **wear** clothes, they cover part of your body.
2 If something **wears** out, it becomes less useful because it has been used so much. *Maggie's shoes are **wearing** out.*

weather
The **weather** is what it is like outside. The weather can be hot or cold, rainy or sunny.

web
webs
A **web** is a very thin net that a spider makes to catch insects.

we'd
1 We'd is a short way of saying we had. *We'd just reached the forest when it started to rain.*
2 We'd is also a short way of saying we would. *We'd love to come to your party.*

wedding
weddings
When a man and woman have a **wedding**, they get married.

weed
weeds
A **weed** is a wild plant. *Mom is trying to get rid of the **weeds** in our yard.*

week
weeks
A **week** is a period of seven days. There are fifty-two weeks in a year.

weekend
weekends
A **weekend** is Saturday and Sunday. *We often go biking on **weekends**.*

weep
weeps weeping wept
When you **weep**, tears come from your eyes because you are sad. *Hector wept when his rat escaped.*

weigh
weighs weighing weighed
When you **weigh** something or someone, you find out how heavy they are. *Marty **weighed** the fish he had caught. Carmen **weighed** herself on the scale.*

weight
weights
Your **weight** is how heavy you are. *Do you know your **weight**?*

welcome
welcomes welcoming welcomed
If you **welcome** someone, you are friendly to them when they arrive. *We rushed outside to welcome Grandpa.*

well
wells
A **well** is a deep hole in the ground. People dig wells to reach water, oil or gas.

well
better best
1 If you are **well**, you are healthy. *Brad is looking very **well**.*
2 If you do something **well**, you are good at it. *Leroy plays the violin **well**.*

we'll
We'll is a short way of saying we will. *We'll see you next weekend.*

went
Went comes from the word **go**. *Carolyn likes to go to the beach. She **went** there last week with some friends.*

were
Were comes from the word **be**. *The children tried to be quiet. They **were** silent for two minutes.*

we're
We're is a short way of saying we are. *We're going on vacation tomorrow.*

weren't
Weren't is a short way of saying were not. *We **weren't** allowed to stay up late.*

west
West is a direction. The sun goes down in the west.

wet
wetter wettest
If something is **wet**, it is full of water or covered with water. *A **wet** towel.*
■ opposite **dry**

we've
We've is a short way of saying we have. *We've been playing lots of games.*

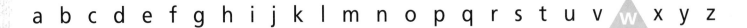

a b c d e f g h i j k l m n o p q r s t u v w x y z

For Internet links, go to
www.usborne-quicklinks.com
139
whale to **wh**o'll

whale
whales
A **whale** is a very big animal that lives in the ocean. A whale breathes through a hole in the top of its head.

what
You use the word **what** to find out more about something. *What is your name?*

what's
What's is a short way of saying **what is**. *What's the time?*

wheat
Wheat is a plant that is grown on farms. Wheat is used to make flour.

wheel
wheels
A **wheel** is round and can turn in a circle. Cars, bicycles and roller skates have wheels.

wheelbarrow
wheelbarrows
You use a **wheelbarrow** to carry things in the yard. A wheelbarrow has a wheel at the front and handles, so that you can push it along.

wheelchair
wheelchairs
A **wheelchair** is a chair on wheels. People who cannot walk use a wheelchair to get from place to place.

wheeze
wheezes wheezing wheezed
When people **wheeze**, they find it hard to breathe.

when
You use the word **when** to ask about the time that something happened. ***When** did you last see Mark?*

where
You use the word **where** to ask about a place. ***Where** are you?*

which
You use the word **which** to ask about one of a number of things. ***Which** shirt shall I wear?*

while
1 **While** means a period of time. *I've waited a long **while** for you.*
2 **While** also means in the time that something is happening. *Sam fed my cat **while** I was away.*

whiskers
Whiskers are the long hairs that grow near the mouth of some animals, such as mice, cats and rabbits. *My pet mouse has very long **whiskers**.*

whisper
whispers whispering whispered
When you **whisper**, you talk very quietly.

whistle
whistles
A **whistle** is a small tube that makes a high, loud sound when you blow into it.

whistle
whistles whistling whistled
When you **whistle**, you make a sound or a tune by blowing through your lips.

white
White is a color. Snow is white.

who
You use the word **who** to ask questions about people. ***Who** won the race?*

who'd
1 **Who'd** is a short way of saying **who had**. *Rosa was the only one **who'd** seen the movie.*
2 **Who'd** is also a short way of saying **who would**. ***Who'd** like to come?*

whole
Whole means all of something. *Zachary has eaten a **whole** bag of cookies.*

who'll
Who'll is a short way of saying **who will**. ***Who'll** come with me?*

why

You use the word **why** to ask about the reason for something. *Why are you upset?*

wicked

Someone who is **wicked** is very bad. *A **wicked** witch.*

wide

wider widest

1 If something is **wide**, it measures a lot from one side to the other. *A **wide** table.*
■ **opposite narrow**
2 If you measure how **wide** something is, you find out how far it is from one side to the other.

width

widths

The **width** of something is how much it measures from one side to the other.

wife

wives

A man's **wife** is the woman he is married to.

wig

wigs

A **wig** is false hair that fits on someone's head.

wild

wilder wildest

Wild animals and plants are not looked after by people.

wildlife

Wildlife is a name for wild animals, insects and plants.

will

would

If you **will** do something, you are going to do it. *I **will** clean up later.*

willing

If you are **willing** to do something, you are happy to do it.

win

wins winning won

If you **win** a race or a game, you come in first.

wind

Wind is air that moves quickly. *The **wind** blew Kelly's hat off.*
▲ *rhymes with pinned*

wind

winds winding wound

1 If you **wind** something around another thing, you put it around it several times. *Alison **wound** her scarf around her neck.*
2 When you **wind** up a clock or a toy, you turn its key to make it work.
3 When roads and rivers **wind**, they have lots of bends and turns.
▲ *rhymes with kind*

windmill

windmills

A **windmill** is a tall building with large sails. When the wind turns the sails, a machine inside the windmill turns grain into flour.

window

windows

A **window** is a space in a building or a vehicle that lets in light and air. Windows are usually filled with glass.

wing

wings

Wings make things able to fly. Birds, insects and airplanes all have wings.

wink

winks winking winked

When you **wink**, you close and open one eye very quickly. You wink to show that something is a joke or a secret.

winner

winners

The **winner** of a race or a game is the person who comes in first.

winter

Winter is one of the four seasons of the year. It comes between fall and spring. In winter, the weather is cold.

wipe

wipes wiping wiped

When you **wipe** something, you rub it with a cloth to make it clean.

wire

wires

A **wire** is a long, thin piece of metal that bends easily. Wires can be used to carry electricity or to hold things together.

wise
wiser wisest
Wise people know the right thing to say and do.

wish
wishes wishing wished
If you **wish** that something would happen, you want it to happen very much.

witch
witches
A **witch** is a woman with magic powers who you read about in stories.

with
1 If you do something **with** someone, you both do it together.
2 You also use the word **with** to show that someone has something. *I know a boy **with** green eyes.*
3 The word **with** also shows what you use to do something. *Natasha loves eating chicken **with** her fingers.*

without
If you are **without** something, you do not have it. *Max came to school **without** his lunch money.*

wizard
wizards
A **wizard** is a man with magic powers who you read about in stories.

wobble
wobbles wobbling wobbled
If something **wobbles**, it moves gently from side to side. *The dessert **wobbled** on the plate.*

woke
Woke comes from the word **wake**. *Anne usually wakes up early, but today she **woke** late.*

wolf

wolves
A **wolf** is a wild animal that looks like a large dog. Wolves have thick coats. They live in forests and hunt in groups.

woman
women
A **woman** is an adult, female human being.

won
Won comes from the word **win**. *Our team hopes to win today. We have **won** our last five games.*

wonder
wonders wondering wondered
1 If you **wonder** what to do, you are not sure what you should do.
2 If you **wonder** about something, you think about it because you are curious. *Karen **wondered** what was in the box.*

won't
Won't is a short way of saying will not. *Meg **won't** let her brother come into her room.*

wood
woods
Wood comes from the trunk and branches of trees. It is used to make things, such as furniture and paper.

woods
A place where lots of trees grow is called the **woods**. *We went for a walk in the **woods**.*

wooden
Something that is **wooden** is made from wood. *A **wooden** spoon.*

wool
Wool is the hair that grows on sheep. Wool is made into yarn and used for knitting or making cloth.

word
words
A **word** is a group of sounds or letters that means something. You use words when you speak or write.

wore
Wore comes from the word **wear**. *Kim didn't know what to wear. In the end, she **wore** her jeans.*

work
works working worked
1 When people **work**, they do a job. *My mom **works** in a hospital.*
2 If you **work**, you use your energy to do something. *Mercedes is **working** hard on her homework.*
3 If something **works**, it does what it is meant to do. *Our radio is **working** again.*

world
The **world** is the planet on which we live. The world is also called the earth. *I'd love to travel around the **world**.*

worm
worms
A **worm** is a small creature with a long, thin body and no legs. Worms live in the ground.

worn
Worn comes from the word **wear**. *Emily likes to wear big hats. She has **worn** that hat every day this week.*

worry
worries worrying worried
If you **worry**, you keep
thinking about bad things
that might happen.

worse
Worse means less good. *Your
handwriting is **worse** than mine.*

worst
Worst means worse than anything
else. *This is the **worst** movie I have
ever seen.*
■ *opposite* **best**

worth
If something is **worth** an amount
of money, it can be sold for that
amount. *This painting is **worth** a
lot of money.*

would
Would comes from the word will.
*I will come to see you this week.
I **would** have come last week, but
I was busy.*

wouldn't
Wouldn't is a short way of saying
would not. *Becky **wouldn't** lend
her brother any money.*

wound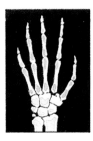
wounds
A **wound** is a cut in your skin. *You
need a bandage on that **wound**.*
▲ *rhymes with spooned*

wound
Wound comes from the word
wind. *Jo started to wind the yarn.
She **wound** it around her hand.*
▲ *rhymes with sound*

wrap
wraps wrapping wrapped
When you **wrap** an object, you
cover it with something, such as
paper or cloth. *Todd **wrapped**
Eric's present in red paper.*

wrapper
wrappers

A **wrapper** is a piece of
paper or plastic
that covers
something.
*A candy **wrapper**.*

wreck
wrecks wrecking wrecked
If you **wreck** something, you
completely destroy it. *My brother
has **wrecked** my radio, so I can't
listen to it any more.*

wrestle
wrestles wrestling wrestled
When people **wrestle**, they fight
and try to throw each other to
the ground.

wrinkle
wrinkles
A **wrinkle** is a line on someone's
skin. *The old man's face was
covered with **wrinkles**.*

wrist
wrists
Your **wrist** is the joint between
your arm and your hand.

write
writes writing wrote written
1 When you **write**, you use a pen
or pencil to put words or numbers
on paper.
2 When you **write** a story, you
make it up. *Amanda is **writing** a
story about a dragon.*

writing
Writing is anything that has been
written.

written
Written comes from the word
write. *Holly writes to Ali regularly.
She has **written** every week since
she moved away.*

wrong
1 If people do something **wrong**,
they do something bad.
2 Something that is **wrong** is not
correct. *Some of my answers
were **wrong**.*
■ *opposite* **right**

wrote
Wrote comes from the word
write. *David likes to write poems.
Last week, he **wrote** a poem
about a tiger.*

Xx

x-ray
x-rays
An **x-ray** is a kind
of photograph
that shows the
inside of
someone's body.

xylophone
xylophones
A **xylophone** is a musical
instrument with a row of wooden
bars. You play a xylophone
by hitting the bars
with small
hammers.
▲ *say
zy-loh-fone*

Yy

yard
yards
A **yard** is a piece of land around a house. *The children are playing in the yard.*

yarn
Yarn is thread made from wool. People knit with yarn.

yawn

yawns yawning yawned
When you **yawn**, you open your mouth wide and breathe in deeply. You yawn because you are tired or bored.

year
years
A **year** is a period of 12 months.

yell
yells yelling yelled
If you **yell**, you shout or scream very loudly. *Mike yelled for help.*

yellow
Yellow is a color. Lemons and butter are yellow.

yesterday
Yesterday was the day before today. *Yesterday we went to the circus.*

yogurt
Yogurt is a thick liquid that is made from milk. Yogurt is often sold in cartons.

yolk
yolks
The **yolk** is the yellow part in the middle of an egg.

— yolk

you
You is a word that you use when you speak to someone else. *How are you feeling?*

you'd
1 **You'd** is a short way of saying you had. *You'd already left when I came by.*
2 **You'd** is also a short way of saying you would. *You'd have enjoyed the party.*

you'll
You'll is a short way of saying you will. *You'll be cold if you don't wear a coat.*

young
younger youngest
Someone who is **young** has lived for only a short time.
■ *opposite* **old**

you're
You're is a short way of saying you are. *You're late again!*

yourself
Yourself means you and nobody else. *Help yourself to some food.*

you've
You've is a short way of saying you have. *You've eaten far too much cake!*

yo-yo
yo-yos
A **yo-yo** is a toy that rolls up and down on a string that you loop around your finger.

Zz

zebra
zebras
A **zebra** is an animal with black and white stripes on its body. Zebras look like horses and live in herds.

zero
Zero is the number 0. When you take away two from two you get zero.

zigzag
zigzags
A **zigzag** is a line which goes up and down.

zipper
zippers
Zippers are sewn into clothes and bags and are used to fasten them. A zipper has two rows of metal or plastic teeth which fit together when you pull it up.

zoo
zoos
A **zoo** is a place where wild animals are kept for people to see.

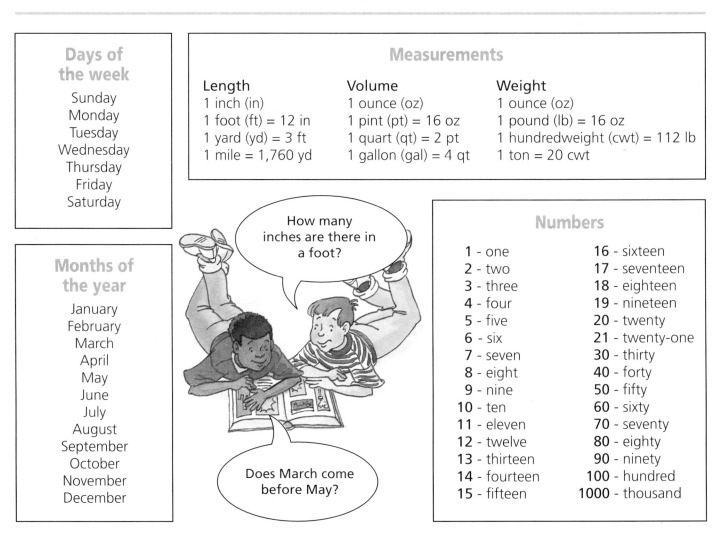

Days of the week

Sunday
Monday
Tuesday
Wednesday
Thursday
Friday
Saturday

Months of the year

January
February
March
April
May
June
July
August
September
October
November
December

Measurements

Length	Volume	Weight
1 inch (in)	1 ounce (oz)	1 ounce (oz)
1 foot (ft) = 12 in	1 pint (pt) = 16 oz	1 pound (lb) = 16 oz
1 yard (yd) = 3 ft	1 quart (qt) = 2 pt	1 hundredweight (cwt) = 112 lb
1 mile = 1,760 yd	1 gallon (gal) = 4 qt	1 ton = 20 cwt

How many inches are there in a foot?

Does March come before May?

Numbers

1 - one	16 - sixteen
2 - two	17 - seventeen
3 - three	18 - eighteen
4 - four	19 - nineteen
5 - five	20 - twenty
6 - six	21 - twenty-one
7 - seven	30 - thirty
8 - eight	40 - forty
9 - nine	50 - fifty
10 - ten	60 - sixty
11 - eleven	70 - seventy
12 - twelve	80 - eighty
13 - thirteen	90 - ninety
14 - fourteen	100 - hundred
15 - fifteen	1000 - thousand

Answers to puzzles

page 3   **Alphabetical animals**: bear, beaver, caterpillar, chicken, chimpanzee, crab, crocodile.

page 4   **Which word?**: 1 mouse, 2 fish, 3 shallow, 5 marble, 7 motorcyle, 8 musical instruments.
What am I?: kite, ring, air, bike, book.

page 5   **Adding words:** One hot day, a thirsty crow called Caspar was searching for something to drink. The stream had dried up and there was no water anywhere. / In the distance, Caspar saw a pitcher on a table outside a cottage. He flew over to have a look. "Ah, there's water at the bottom," he said. But he could not reach it. Caspar felt more and more thirsty. He tried to push over the pitcher, but it was so heavy that he could not move it. / Then he had an idea. He flew off to a pile of pebbles and picked one up in his beak. Caspar flew back, dropped a pebble into the pitcher and then went off to find another. He dropped so many pebbles into the pitcher that they pushed the water up to the top. At last, he could have a long, cool drink. "All my hard work was worth it in the end," thought clever Caspar.

The publishers are grateful to the following for lending items to be photographed:
Boots (21); Boswells, Oxford (18, 45, 62, 114, 139); British Home Stores (63); Cardew and Company (124); Early Learning Centre (23, 29, 48, 81, 113); Habitat (13, 18, 31, 43, 45, 74, 75, 90, 92, 135); H. Samuel (137); Lewis's (14, 43, 48, 102); Marks and Spencer (112); Mitsui Machinery Sales (UK) (73); New for Knitting, Oxford (62, 141, 143); Next (59, 108, 136); Oddballs Juggling and Kite Company, Oxford (61); Oxford Cheese Company (24); Pennyfarthing Cycle Centre, Oxford (92); Restore, Oxford (130); RPB Warehouse, Oxford (25, 81, 84, 114, 133); Russell Acott, Oxford (36, 74); Tool Club, Oxford (11, 123); Toys Я Us (29); Two Foot Nothing, Oxford (121); Yamaha-Kemble Music (UK) (96); YHA Adventure (27).